The Reference Realist
in Library Academia

# THE REFERENCE REALIST IN LIBRARY ACADEMIA

## Patricia Gebhard

McFarland & Company, Inc., Publishers
*Jefferson, North Carolina, and London*

British Library Cataloguing-in-Publication data are available

Library of Congress Cataloguing-in-Publication Data

Gebhard, Patricia.
    The reference realist in library academia / Patricia Gebhard.
      p.  cm.
    Includes bibliographical references and index.
    ISBN 0-7864-0237-7 (library binding : 50# alkaline paper) ∞
    1.  Academic libraries—Reference services—United States.
  I. Title
  Z675.U5G395   1997
  025.5'277—dc21                    96-46874
                                     CIP

Manufactured in the United States of America

*McFarland & Company, Inc., Publishers
  Box 611, Jefferson, North Carolina 28640*

# Contents

# Acknowledgments

I am indebted :

To the UCSB Davidson library for providing me the opportunity to learn what it means to be a reference librarian. To Don Fitch who let me run with the ball without always tackling me. To Carol Gibbens who provided the ultimate model of the excellent reference librarian. To Patricia Cronshaw and Euzetta Williams for reading the manuscript and making suggestions for improvements. To Connie Dowell for reading the manuscript and encouraging me. To Barbara Silver who could be relied on to give a different perspective on reference services and who insisted I try to include what will be happening in reference service tomorrow. The text reflects my personal perspective on reference, and if it has errors or misunderstandings or indeed insights, they are my responsibility.

# Preface

The intention of this book is to inform the neophyte librarian, the library school student or someone contemplating becoming a librarian about what exactly it means to be a reference librarian in an academic library.

The aim of reference librarians has always been, and continues to be, to help students, faculty and staff to make use of the vast resources in an academic library. But the ways in which librarians provide this assistance evolve continuously and have changed greatly in the 1980s and 1990s. The changes have resulted primarily from the introduction of new technology, an ever present shortage of funds, and a fuller acceptance of partnership with the faculty in the education of students. In discussing the reference activities that may take place in an academic library, the present text will document the impact of recent changes on each of those activities and will propose some strategies for coping with a changing reference environment in the future.

When some librarians recently applied total quality management theory to libraries, they concluded that if reference librarians are needed, the library is inefficient in serving its clients' needs.[1] They see reference librarians as corrective measures and evidently would like a library to operate entirely without them.

The rebuttal to these librarians claims rather that it is inefficient for a library to provide for all unknown needs of the future, and that it is better to assist users whose needs are known when the assistance is provided.[2] I will go even further to assert that reference librarians are the moving force in a library in providing efficiently for the users of academic libraries. It would seem obvious that there will always be students who need help in making their way through the complexities of using a modern library, either through personal contact or through all the self-help devices that reference librarians provide. The challenge for the reference librarian has always been, and continues to be, how best to assist the users of the library.

This book approaches the question of how future library users will be helped by first considering how they have been helped in the past and are being helped at the present moment. It in some measure documents how librarians have confronted and resolved problems in the library that have necessitated changes. It shows how the active, inquisitive minds of reference librarians have made it possible for them to adapt to present day challenges and to work out ways of adapting in the future. It indicates how librarians have made sure, and will continue to make sure, that the students, faculty and staff in an academic library receive the service which reference librarians believe in.

# PART I.

# Direct Assistance

Reference work in the academic library has been defined as direct personal service to library users in fulfilling their needs for information through the use of library resources. But a more inclusive definition is now needed to encompass everything a reference librarian does to assist the user. Restated, reference work is the service activities of reference librarians which insure that users of the library are successful in obtaining the information which they need or want from the library. The use of technology has not changed this basic purpose of reference service. Users on a university campus will continue to need information and help finding it.

Even though other means of helping users have increased in importance, direct personal service remains the main way in which reference librarians assist their users. Thus, the discussion starts with direct personal service. Originally, personal service meant that librarians assisted students at a service point (or desk) when they asked for help. Now, personal service may be given when librarians identify students with search problems, when students are referred to librarians from another service point, when librarians are on standby and are called to give assistance or when they have made an appointment with students to assist them.

The discussion, which follows, on the interaction between librarians and users in satisfying users' needs applies regardless of the location of the interaction, but since reference librarians still consider desk service their top priority, the discussion will mainly be from the perspective of requests originating at service desks.

The first few days on a reference desk for a new librarian can be pretty scary, enough that even now the author remembers the feeling of wanting to run to the nearest experienced librarian for help with each new question. As Anderson states it, "Standing behind a desk labeled 'Information' or 'Reference,' offering to all comers 'The Answer' to their question—dealing with wildly varying subjects as frequently as every three or four minutes—is a stressful occupation, in case you hadn't noticed."[1]

New librarians soon discover, as the author did, that despite their inexperiences, even they know more about how to access information in the library than users do. Thus, after a short time, while a twinge of anxiety may still accompany the approach of each student, the new librarian will soon feel comfortable assisting students.

This section on the reference transaction provides the new librarian with suggestions for working with students and includes references to articles which may discuss some parts of the transaction in greater depth. By considering what is presented and trying the suggestions, over time, librarians will learn to make the decisions which help users the most. Over time is important to keep in mind because it may take several years for new reference librarians to become truly proficient at their jobs.[2]

On the surface, personal service at a desk seems a simple matter. A student comes up to a reference librarian and is greeted in a friendly way. He explains his request, and the librarian directs the student to a reference source or identifies a relevant book or periodical article for him. Voila! the student finds references to articles or facts in a source which looks perfect for his request or finds a book or periodical in the library collections. The student obtains his material and happily leaves the library to work on his paper.

But in actual fact the encounter is more complicated than it appears and is full of possibilities for success or failure from before the librarian's first smile until the student moves to the book stacks. Reference encounters are complex, multi-faceted transactions requiring many decisions. If reference librarians consciously considered all these decisions, they would hardly be able to operate at all. To understand the decision-making process, it is helpful to consider the reference encounter as a series of steps.

Thus, following the path of others, the reference transaction is discussed as a series of steps: conducting an interview, designing a search strategy, identifying sources, making use of sources identified, and completing the transaction.[3] By analyzing these steps, librarians can understand the reference process and develop standards through which service can be improved and failure prevented.

*Chapter 1.*

# The Interview

The interaction between a student[1] and a librarian begins with what has been called an interview. The point of the interview is for the reference librarian to discover the best way to assist the student in satisfying the needs which brought the student to the librarian for help. The interview is a verbal exchange which can be very brief or quite extensive.

The interaction between the librarian and the student begins before the first word is spoken. Students react to the nonverbal signals of librarians and continue to be aware of these signals during an interchange. A student will be encouraged to request help if a librarian appears friendly, approachable and not too involved with something at the desk which the student might think she is interrupting. If a librarian looks directly at a student, perhaps stands and walks toward her or just leans a little toward her, the student will conclude that the librarian is ready to give attention to the request for assistance.

These examples of elements in approachability are just a few of the nonverbal clues that have been ascertained to operate in a reference encounter.[2] Other nonverbal communication features of an encounter might be physical distance and relationship, posture, head nodding, facial expression, eye contact, gestures and all the ways in which the voice can be used to convey meaning beyond the words.

Librarians can learn good nonverbal communication skills in library school or in workshop programs and put them into practice to improve their ability to relate in a positive way to students.[3] Undoubtedly, a good reference librarian will naturally display these nonverbal characteristics which indicate to the student that the librarian is a non-threatening person, eager to help. One librarian had great success with a student merely by stating quite frankly that she was friendly.

Librarians for their own part tend to evaluate students before the purposes for their requests are stated. While librarians may find it useful to identify students as undergraduates, graduate students or faculty members when they approach, it is more important to detect whether the students are self-assured, whether they have an assignment in hand, or whether it will be easy to establish rapport with them.

One of the challenges of assisting students is to meet each one with the same degree of enthusiasm. It simply is not possible to have rapport with everyone. A librarian may need to make a conscious effort to assist the unmotivated or disagreeable student with the same degree of helpfulness as the student who attracts the librarian. Generally, most librarians can work with a student regardless of negative interpersonal dynamics.

Handling the problem patron is a completely different situation from mere rapport. While the difficult patron is more commonly found in public libraries, the academic librarian may have patrons who are mentally disturbed or aggressive. The academic library should have rules about unacceptable behavior posted and available to the librarian, who must make a decision about what to do, including when to call the campus police. Some academic libraries will have security officers within the building.[4] As with problem patrons, bomb threats will require rules for action.[5]

For an interview, librarians may initiate the encounter with the student by saying "May I help you?" or "How may I help you?" or just by giving the appearance of being available or by walking toward the student. Students may initiate the encounter by saying "I need..." or "I am looking for..." or "I have an assignment..."

The student's query may be quite straightforward and easily satisfied—a simple locational question, an easily understood request for the identification of sources, or an assignment that the librarian has encountered previously. It has been determined in studies that half of the requests for information require very little in terms of an interview.[6]

If the librarian cannot immediately determine a course of action for answering a question, he will have to get as much detail as possible about what it is that the student is actually seeking. The librarian must gather enough information about the request and requester to plan how best the library system can fulfill the student's need.[7] New librarians may not understand why students frame their questions the way they do, but they will soon discover that they must often go beyond the question asked to determine what the student really wants.

What does a librarian need to find out from the questions she poses to student? To begin with, the subject of the request and what information is needed about the subject. If the librarian does not immediately recognize the subject of the request, she may have to ask the student more about it, make use of a reference source such as an encyclopedia or dictionary, or even ask a colleague about the subject. Examples of subjects for which the librarian might need more information might be yellow dog contracts, causes of aphasia or special curves. The librarian will also ask the student what he wants to find out about the subject.

In the process of talking with the student, the librarian will make a judgment about the student in terms of library sophistication (Can he use the on-line catalog? Does he know what is meant by CD-ROM?)[8], or reading ability and language facility (Does the student read the language in which much of the information is written?).[9] The librarian will have to determine how much time and effort the student is willing to devote to finding a solution, and in what format the student hopes to find the information. It is possible to ascertain much of this information without asking directly for it. Perhaps the best way to find out what the student needs to know is to ask the student why she needs the information.

Some reference librarians feel that they never should ask patrons why they need the information, believing that to ask is an invasion of the patron's privacy or is rude.[10] Perhaps in a public library it is not appropriate to ask, but in an academic library, the reasons for information requests are likely to be course related and thus not too sensitive to be explained to librarians.

It is easier to develop a plan of action to assist students in finding information if one knows why the information is needed.[11] Without prying, the librarian can determine that the reason for the question is a class assignment and can thus inquire further about the due date and the information needed. Because librarians handle questions involving a small amount of information differently from those associated with a long paper, it is helpful to know the extent of the assignment.

Because students are unaware of what librarians know about their specific subjects, they quite often couch their questions in general terms as a starting point.[12] Reference librarians will have to ask a series of questions to hone in on the "real" question, seeking to establish a meeting between their own concepts about the library and those of the students.[13]

Once the librarian and student have reached a rapport and a mutual understanding about the library, and the student has a reasonable assurance that the librarian will be able to help, the student will be more open in answering the questions the librarian may ask to determine more specifically what the student is looking for. From the experience of working with a reference librarian, the student may state his request more directly another time.

On the other hand, some students ask for a specific reference source with which they are acquainted. Reference librarians will have to make a judgment on these requests: Should they simply direct the students to the requested source or should they find out what is needed? Often librarians use the question and statement, "What exactly are you looking for? That may not be the best place to look." Some students may be adamant, repeating their request for the reference source location. Some may be happy to explain their problem because they were groping in the first place. Librarians must also be willing to accept that indeed, in some cases, the sources requested are the best places to look. In these cases, the librarians can make the students feel good about their ability to use the library rather than thinking, "I muffed that one." Considerable tact is required when an instructor has referred students to an inappropriate source or an inaccurate citation.

Another instance of the need for tact is when the librarian must explain to the student why the question has no answer: an explanation, for example, of why the student will not be able to find statistics on unreported rape or why it is necessary to look under a more general heading if the first heading produces little or no information.

Tact must be used in the whole setting of the reference desk. Librarians will need to decide in which order to help students. They will have to develop ways of making sure that the students do not feel they are waiting too long or are abandoned. Before walking away from the desk to work on a longer question, the librarian could ask the waiting students if their questions are "quickies." Why ask students to wait even two or three minutes if all they want to know is where a specific source is located or some other information as easily answered?

It should not matter to the librarian that many of these quickies are locational or informational questions that might easily have been answered at an information desk. Even without making use of the "quickie" question with students, librarians can acknowledge students by a nod of the head or by saying "I'll be right with you." Deciding how to help students when there is a line at the desk is one of the decisions a librarian is required to make in an effort to serve students equitably.

When two librarians are scheduled on a desk, it is perhaps better to let misguidance occur than for one librarian to intervene in answering a question put to the other, unless he can add something essential, is sure he is correct, and will not cause the other librarian to lose face with the patron.

In Hawley's study of referral, some of the librarians used tact at the expense of the user to such an extent that the user suffered.[14] Olszak discusses how a librarian can correct her colleagues in a tactful way so that mistakes are not made.[15] The issue is one of effective staff training and should be addressed.

Librarians can handle the problem of not agreeing with a colleague's answers in various ways. A librarian can discuss the inquiry with his partner after the student has gone away. The reaction may be a simple "Oh, I forgot about that," a lively discussion about which sources are best for which topics, or a more prickly response.

It is also possible to surreptitiously approach students and steer them to more satisfactory sources than recommended by a colleague. And if it is an on-line catalog students are fretting with, librarians can approach them to verify their success in quite a legitimate way without the other librarian feeling his question has been taken over.

## Interviewing Techniques

Basically, librarians ask questions in an interview to discover what they need to know. They will have to figure out the type of questions to ask and in which order. They will have to figure out what information being offered should be pursued, what type of feedback to provide (i.e., how to reply to the student's questions) and what digressions will work in obtaining and maintaining a user's cooperation.[16]

Because each request may be a separate problem, librarians will have "to know and use a wide range of approaches and skills during the interview."[17] It is to be hoped that interviewing skills will be learned in library schools, but it is useful for even skilled librarians to attend workshops on technique. For those with inadequate techniques, workshops or mentoring by skilled librarians will be essential. Librarians usually develop an interviewing style of their own based on many techniques.

Questions asked of the student are basically of two types: closed, in which the questions are answered yes or no, or open, in which the librarian asks for an explanation of what is needed. Closed questions are restrictive in nature, usually limiting the options to yes or no answers or a choice between two or more alternatives. Librarians use closed questions extensively because they readily narrow searches.[18] In a way, by asking closed questions, one can make an educated guess about what the patron needs.

The problem in using closed questions comes when students cannot answer questions yes or no. If they cannot, librarians may have to back up and start over again using open questions or other alternatives. Librarians are in a position to use closed questions if they know exactly what the assignment is or have a thorough knowledge of the subject. Sometimes, they can more quickly move toward a search strategy by asking closed questions.

Perhaps the least effective type of closed question is to ask the students whether they have looked in a specific source because they may not have the vaguest idea what the librarian is talking about. Chances are students would not be asking for assistance if they had tried the reference tool suggested by the reference librarian. A better question is, "Where have you looked already?"

Open questions provide an opportunity for the student to explain his subject. Through the student's explanations, the librarian will readily pick up concepts to be used for searching. Open questions can help students clarify in their own minds exactly what they want if they have started out with an ill-defined subject.

There are ways of avoiding premature diagnosing of the problem. One of the ways is a refinement of open questions, the use of neutral questions. As Dervin explains, "The neutral questioning strategy directs the librarian to learn from the user the nature of the underlying situation, the gaps faced, and the expected uses."[19] In neutral questioning, librarians see the question from the user's point of view rather than leading the user to their determination of what is needed. They allow students to say what they really want. Using neutral questions, librarians will gain an understanding of what the situation is, the information needed, and the use to be made of the information. Because the librarian will have a fuller description of the user's informational need, she will be more helpful.

The idea of finding evidence (rather than information) for a student paper may be elucidated by neutral questioning so that the question becomes, "What evidence do you need to support the hypothesis of your project?"

Neutral questioning is similar to Allen's text structure questions in which the student is asked about what kind of information he expects to find and in what format. The question for the student would be, "What findings do you expect to be reported in the articles we locate?"[20] Allen's study shows that if students posit for librarians the type of study they are looking for in terms of methodology and results, librarians will be more successful in assisting the student because they have a wider range of suggestions for strategy and subjects to use for searching than if they merely determine the overall subject of the search and synonyms for the subject. [21]

Another technique of an open type to elicit what the student really needs is to rephrase what the student has requested. By rephrasing the request, librarians indicate to students that the request is understood. Generally, with rephrasing students will volunteer the reason for the request and explain more specifically what is needed.[22]

Interviews are conducted to determine the appropriate level of service for the student. In any given situation, librarians do not usually plan to use any particular type of question, but simply choose questions to find out enough about the request to assist the student. The best questions are those that make possible the most efficient way of redefining the request in terms of library resources.

The interview, but not the transaction, ends when the librarian has sufficient information about what is needed to determine the sources likely to provide the information on a level that fits the ability and interest of the student.

# Chapter 2.
# Search Strategy

At the next step, the librarian works out strategies for answering the student's informational need. Basically the strategies are plans for action. While the interview was presented as a distinct step, in actual fact the second step, the development of a search strategy, may occur simultaneously with the first. Librarians usually operate on two or three levels in their minds while assisting students. While they talk with students about what they are looking for, they may be actively considering and ranking possible sources. This is a bit tricky because librarians need to be fully attentive to what students are saying, but it happens and is helpful.

In fact, as part of determining what students want, librarians may consult sources—for example, an online catalog—as they speak with students. Librarians might start to walk with patrons to possible sources while discussing the query.

Search strategy is the translation of queries into the language of the library system so that the query is satisfied. Search strategy is "a conscious approach to decision making to achieve specific objectives."[1] Before recommendations are made, the librarian must have the parameters of the query clearly in mind, as well as the subject, time available, geographic area if there is one, and the date of the information needed.

On the basis of what they know about the request, librarians decide where the user should look for information and in what sequence. Having determined a source, librarians make sure the students can locate the source and know how to use it. New librarians will have already learned a great deal about matching questions to sources in library school or through their initial training on the job.[2]

In the process of developing a search strategy, librarians will categorize queries in their minds in order to more easily figure out a way of attacking the problem. Questions can be broken down into a wide range of categories or types when viewed from various angles.

Derr has suggested that there are two parts to patrons' questions, the subject and the query (the latter being defined as what is asked *about* the subject; i.e., what the patron needs to know about the subject).[3] He sets up eight categories of questions that can be asked about subjects based on concepts inherent in them: existence, identity, properties, relation, number, location, time and action. His concepts are especially useful for factual questions.

The criteria that Piternick has set up for determining when to use an online search or when to use printed tools, like Derr's list of concepts, are categories which may be useful to consider for any strategy.[4]

Instead of categories, White refers to frames in both the users' and librarians' minds which provide the basis for understanding between them. She uses the frames to develop a model for analyzing interviews.[5] Frames give insight into the mental processes of librarians.

Frames are substantial structures of stereotyped situations in long term memory which are called up as needed for specific instances. The frames are also joined into frame sets which make it possible to link the frames quickly. As with the categories, if the librarian has a frame for the question he can assist the student with greater alacrity. Mind frames can make it possible for a librarian to proceed with helping a student without extensive questioning. Frames sometimes make interview tapes used for evaluation difficult to analyze for content because they do not show up on the tape.

Here are some examples. Both student and librarian will have an interview frame. The librarian will have a user frame. Librarians will have a student motivation frame "writing a paper." For a useful frame, White uses a specific school assignment.[6] For example, with a frame for a case law class assignment, the librarian could simply ask "Which case have you been assigned?"

Categories and frames explain how librarians rapidly determine how to satisfy a student's request for information. They present the librarian with possibilities for searching and may also suggest priorities and value judgments on sources.

In presenting strategies for searching, this discussion makes use of four types of questions, within which there may be possibilities for further categorization: informational and locational questions, known item requests, factual and simple subject searches, and substantive subject searches.

## 1. Informational and Locational Questions

The most basic questions asked in a library are queries about library locations, services or hours. Because they do not require any depth of knowledge or problem solving skills, they can be fielded by paraprofessionals at an information desk. (The use of paraprofessionals will discussed in the section on reference desk support.) Even if there is an information desk, some students will still ask these questions at the reference desk. It is important that reference librarians answer even these simple questions courteously and informatively because they can affect the way these inquirers will view the library throughout their whole college careers.[7]

Locational or informational questions about the library are answered from knowledge of the library or by making use of a desk manual, a published handbook or leaflets on the library.

## 2. Known Item Requests

Known item requests are those in which a student has a definite citation to a book, periodical or other materials. The strategy requires the verification of the citation and the determination of ownership by the library (or, if the source is not owned, the determination that it is in another library and available to the student). A librarian or library assistant helps the student in using the catalog for the library (card or online) or serials lists or even online catalogs of regional or national databases. The local catalog is, of course, top priority for known item searches whether the catalog is online or in card or printed form.

Where they still exist, card catalogs are searched by means of a set number of entries or access points: author, title, series, and subject. Online catalogs increase the number of access points by providing the possibility of searching by keyword or by other fields in the record such as LC card number or call number.[8] A keyword is any significant word which can be searched in the title or subject fields, for example.

When serial citations are to be verified, they may be identified in the library's catalogs or serials lists, but the record for the serial must include the volumes owned by the library. Librarians may have to help students differentiate the title of the serial from the article title and assist in the interpretation of abbreviated titles. Librarians may make educated guesses about the title, use a number of different abbreviation sources, or with some systems use truncation of the title (i.e., the abbreviation) in searching online. Location of proceedings in a catalog is particularly difficult because of the different ways they may be entered in the catalog. Keyword searching can be especially useful for these.

This second kind of question can, to a certain extent, also be handled on a basic level by well-trained paraprofessionals at an information desk. It requires only a basic understanding of online catalog search protocols. Protocols include the steps which must be performed to reach a database before searching as well as the abbreviations and terms used for searching. In some online public access catalogs, protocols are unnecessary because the catalog presents the user with well explained abbreviations and steps for searching, including further directions during the progress of a search as well as help screens.

Students may, however, have citations for which the information is inaccurate or incomplete, or which present difficult identification problems that require the reference librarian's more thorough knowledge of the catalog. This knowledge includes the rules of entry for all types of material and the fields and tags used for them in the MARC format.

If the librarian finds that the citation is not owned locally with the information available, local or national bibliographic networks can be consulted to determine existence and availability. Both OCLC

(Online Computer Library Center) and RLIN (Research Library Information Network) are huge bibliographic databases made up of Library of Congress MARC tapes and catalog information contributed by member libraries. Besides complete bibliographic information, these databases provide locations of titles in libraries throughout the country as well as interlibrary loan systems for requesting materials found. Originally OCLC was available through dedicated terminals and RLIN by dialing into the computer, but they are now both available through the Internet. FirstSearch, an online interactive search service giving access to a number of databases, is available via OCLC.[9] One of the main databases is WorldCat, OCLC's union catalog with subject access.[10]

The WLN (Western Library Network) and MELVYL (based at the University of California) are local networks rather than national, but they too provide bibliographic information and location of titles. The latter now provides online network access to college and university online library catalogs throughout the country, to the CALLS (California Academic Libraries List of Serials) periodicals database, and to OCLC, making use of its own search abbreviations.

Internet is an international computer telecommunication network. Besides making it possible to use remote online catalogs, Internet makes possible e-mail, forums for discussion, software available in the public domain, and full text information searching. Through its File Transfer Protocol, any information found through Internet can be transferred to the user's computer for downloading.[11]

While much information can be accessed freely, some uses require passwords so that charges can be made above and beyond the dial-up access fee. Providing terminals and training saps the already limited funds of a library.

Because Internet is considered a superhighway, what could be called navigation tools have been developed to assist users. These tools assist users in finding what is available in some cases making use of menus. Examples of these tools are Archie, Gopher, Veronica, and WAIS. To assist the reference librarian, there are books and workshops on Internet use.[12]

Libraries may also, perhaps in the Reference Manual at the desk or in a separate Internet notebook, keep printed lists of library online catalogs, subject guides to discussion groups, directories of electronic journals and newsletters and full texts available.[13] The notebook may also include copies of the articles published in *College & Research Libraries News* on access to various subject fields.[14]

Before the online age, it was possible to verify bibliographic citations but much more difficult to identify location. These printed sources can still be used, but not as easily as online equivalents. In fact, some bibliographies are printed in a microfilm format requiring the use of reading equipment.

For locations in the United States, one may consult the *National Union Catalog, Union List of Serials*, or *New Serials Titles*. Other bibliographies of early works or current bibliographies such as *Books in Print* or *Cumulative Book Index* can be useful for verification. For government publications, there are basic bibliographies as well as the current *Monthly Catalog of United States Government Publications* and *Monthly Checklist of State Publications*. Published bibliographies exist for specialized publications such as society works or dissertations. Most foreign countries have published bibliographies in book form for national libraries or the major libraries in the country.

In suggesting the use of national online databases and printed bibliographies, the assumption is that reference librarians and library assistants will have the ability to use them effectively in finding citations. The interlibrary loan assistants will be the experts on identification and location, but since many interlibrary loan departments require verification of items, reference librarians assist students and faculty in this verification.

Librarians may have to suggest alternative materials for undergraduate students because they do not have the time to wait for their materials. When alternative material is sought, the strategy turns into a subject search as discussed below.

## 3. Factual Information and Simple Subject Searches

Requests for factual information at reference desks may be for succinct data or for more general information about subjects of all sorts: people, places, organizations, flora, fauna, objects, ideas. Factual information of this nature is usually found in reference sources which contain the information itself rather than lead to the information.

It is for factual questions that categories are particularly useful. If students know which source contains the facts they are looking for and know how to use it, they may only ask the librarian about the location of the source. If they do not know sources, students and the librarians who assist them will have to identify which sources contain the information or which group of sources.

Reference collections to a considerable extent are made up of books with files that answer specific factual questions. Here are the major types of reference works in the library which are used for factual and simple informational questions: encyclopedias, dictionaries, almanacs, yearbooks, handbooks, biographical works, critical works, geographical works, and directories. Librarians in searching for information can make an assumption that there should be a reference work that includes the information and then set about trying to determine if one exists. Identification of sources is discussed in the next chapter.

## *4. Subject Searching*

Many reference librarians consider the request for information about a subject the main reason they are reference librarians in an academic library and why they enjoy working on a desk. It is why they appreciate an information desk screening questions and why they are enthusiastic about reference by appointment, particularly in the area of online searching. Librarians need superior bibliographic skills and knowledge of sources in order to help a student with subject inquiries.[15]

Through the interview, the librarian has determined the subject of the request and what the student needs to know about it. The librarian now determines the places to look and in what order depending on such factors as the conditions for the search, the amount of material or currency of information.

## LIBRARY CATALOGS

The library catalog is the first reference source for substantive questions, both for finding actual materials and for finding bibliographies and guides to the literature which may assist the students in their search for information.

Before the advent of keyword searching in an online catalog, librarians often determined the controlled vocabulary of the catalog by using the *Library of Congress Subject Heading List* before searching subject headings. The list provides not only authoritative headings, but also cross references to related, more general or more specific headings. Thus, the list may still be consulted to determine the best subject heading for searching in the catalog. But by using keyword searching users can go directly to the catalog and can use current terminology or synonyms not used in subject headings.

Examples of keywords not found in subject headings include "baby boomers" ("baby boom generation" is the subject heading) or "flower children" ("hippies" is used instead as the subject heading). Authoritative subject headings still are an excellent way to search, however. Once the authoritative heading is found in the record for a book, it may be used to provide more pertinent information for the student.

## BIBLIOGRAPHIES

Librarians frequently recommend bibliographies to students. Indeed subject bibliographies and guides to the literature may be the best sources for students to consult as they begin extensive projects, such as theses or dissertations, because some of the guides provide methodology for the field as well as actual book listings.

Bibliographies can take a number of different forms. Catalogs of libraries are actually bibliographies of what is owned by a given library. National library catalogs or catalogs of specialized collections can be particularly useful for subject searches, especially if they contain periodical citations. Before the advent of national online databases, many specialized libraries had their card catalogs copied and printed.[16] Examples include the catalog of the Peabody Museum for Archaeology and Ethnology and the catalog and index of the Avery Architectural Library (now available online through RLIN).

Bibliographies have been compiled on innumerable subjects, both general and specific. Because of their selectivity and organization, bibliographies can be very useful for students—again, particularly if they contain periodical citations.[17] Bibliographies overlap with periodical indexes when they are published serially and a major portion of their citations consists of periodical articles. Conversely, some sources which are considered periodical indexes may include books, pamphlets and documents as well.

Guides to the literature can be used by librarians and students to identify sources of information or particular books. Subject guides are valuable because they not only contain lists of materials, but discuss "(1) the field as a whole; (2) peculiarities of research (and reference) in the discipline; (3) the place of the subject in the mainstream of knowledge; and (4) various forms which are especially applicable for work in the field, i.e., everything from specialized abstract services to patent guides to sources of unpublished research reports."[18] Guides can be large books or mere leaflets put out by the library. These leaflets are sometimes called pathfinders and may be commercially produced.

## INDEXES TO PERIODICALS

Students will find much of the information they need in periodical literature, particularly if their topic is very current. Librarians help students identify the best index or abstract reference source. With the existence of CD-ROMs in a library, students' questions may be satisfied by determining which CD would be the best one for them to use for periodical literature. Once students identify articles, they must determine whether the library owns the periodical they need.

Basic types of indexes to periodicals are indexes themselves, abstract journals and citation indexes. Indexes usually have one alphabetical listing by subject, author and occasionally title. They are relatively easy to use because the citations are listed directly under the subject headings where students can readily find useful articles.

Abstract journals are indexes to periodicals which include abstracts in the citations and are either arranged by large classes of subject or by consecutive numbers. Indexes of various kinds, depending on the subject, must be used to identify citations. Thus, searching an abstracting index is usually a two step process requiring the use of an index and then finding the citation. It may even require three steps if a thesaurus for the controlled vocabulary of the abstract journal is used prior to searching the index.

Citation indexes in the social sciences, humanities and sciences have several parts. One part lists articles by author giving the author's affiliation and the complete bibliographic citation with the references in the articles listed. Another part is a permuted subject index which can be used to identify articles on subjects. The references in the subject section are to the author listings. There is a citation part which indexes the articles by the authors cited in bibliographies or footnotes. Thus it can be discovered who has cited an article in a given year. By tracing the citations, students can follow the development of ideas from one scholar to the next. The bibliographic citations are identified by types such as review. Because of their interdisciplinary nature, citation indexes are particularly useful. (They and their companion publications such as *Current Contents* have been issued online.)

Librarians should explain to students how they can use the bibliography and footnotes in any of the books and articles for finding further information.

It is never enough simply to identify the best indexes for the students. Librarians must make sure that students understand how to use them and assist them in formulating their subject in the terminology of the source. In determining the correct terms, librarians may have to refer to a thesaurus if it exists, helping the student use it. Interpretation of the citations for the students makes it possible for students to find the works cited in the library.

Reference librarians must determine at what point to leave

students to do their own searching. Should it be when the librarian suggests an index and where it is located, when the librarian shows how the index works, after several promising articles are identified, or even after the librarian shows the student the next step in finding the periodical in the library? To some extent it will depend on how busy the desk is, with the librarian determining how much time she can devote to the patron. As discussed later in the section on manuals, a policy statement can give direction, but the individual librarian will have to apply the policy.

## ONLINE SEARCHING

Instead of searching manually in printed indexes to periodicals, librarians may suggest searching for sources of information, particularly periodical articles, by means of online databases. Searching online has many advantages such as the ability to search the citation information, subject headings and the abstracts by keyword and matching search terms in a way that is not possible in printed indexes.

Librarians can help patrons select a database and then develop a search strategy based on the formatting used in the database. They can explain to the patron the use of controlled and uncontrolled vocabulary and the use of Boolean logic to expand and limit the concepts in the search.[19]

It is difficult to present information about online database searching because the technology is rapidly changing and access to databases varies among different academic libraries. Reference librarians need to know the basics of online searching so that they can adapt that knowledge to what is available in the library where they work.

Databases are provided by vendors such as DIALOG or WILSON-LINE. Librarians dial the vendor's computer, using modems. Information is typed and received on a machine which prints the request and answers, or it may be possible to make use of a TV monitor and printer. Searches can be performed and the results printed at that moment, or the results may be printed later by the vendor and mailed to the library.

Each vendor has its own protocol for logging on to its facility and searching its databases. Many databases also have individual characteristics for searching. Vendors maintain a directory of their databases and information on characteristics of the individual databases, perhaps in loose-leaf notebooks so that changes can be made without having to republish the complete collection. Printed handbooks or guides for searching individual database files have been produced.[20] Examples of individual database characteristics include the way periods of time are searched in *Historical Abstracts* or the way in which geological and geographical information can be searched by map coordinates in *Georef.*

Vendors charge users for computer time used and number of citations found or printed. The cost also varies among the different database producers. Recently vendors have been experimenting with various flat fee arrangements. Government-produced databases are the least expensive, but some private producers like the H.W. Wilson Company also offer their databases at reasonable rates.

Because libraries are charged by vendors for online searching, the library profession faces an uncomfortable policy decision: whether to charge for the service. Libraries have made different choices about charges: free use, set charges, or recovery of costs. Also, since searches are costly in terms of librarians' time, academic libraries have made further decisions about providing everyone with the service or restricting it to their basic clientele. Universities and colleges can refer patrons to the public libraries or commercial search services for searches they are not willing to perform.

Even when they do charge their patrons for online database searches, academic libraries authorize reference librarians to perform some ready reference searching free of charge. Reference librarians usually have guidelines for performing ready reference searches: a dollar cost limit (perhaps up to $10), a printed item limit (five to ten), unavailability or datedness of printed sources, or a demand for quick results within a subject area that is difficult to search.[21] An example of the latter would be searching full texts of newspapers for current topics.

Many database producers now issue their files on CD-ROM. Academic libraries knew their patrons would take advantage of these databases, but faced certain problems which have been solved in several ways. Equipment is one of the first. Computers and printers with paper and ink have to be provided, along with the software to make use of a number of different CD-ROMs. In addition to the cost of the computers and printers are the costs of the CD-ROMs. The money for the purchase of CD-ROMs has to come from already inadequate book budgets or other funds and cannot be passed along to the patron.

Libraries have to decide which databases to buy and whether they can stop subscribing to the printed index. Producers sometimes prevent the dropping of subscriptions by offering package deals for both formats. In fact, it is difficult to determine costs of CD-ROMs ahead of time. As with printed indexes, vendors have varied their prices on the bases of projected usage, number of students, and number of terminals. In the case of CD-ROMs, the price may differ if the discs are to be used individually or on local area networks.[22]

Provision of enough search stations and copies of the CD-ROMs has been solved in various ways, including individual computer stations, stations that use disc packs, and local area networks. For single stations and copies, time limits have been set up and reservations taken. Discs or tapes can be purchased from vendors for use on local networks. Libraries must consider costs of providing CD-ROMs in comparison with other ways of accessing the same information. Librarians as academics must keep technology in perspective, making sure it serves teaching and learning in the academic institution.[23]

Patrons have been enthusiastic about online searching from its inception, but have been limited in its use because of costs. Particularly, undergraduates did not choose to pay for online searches. With the introduction of CD-ROM searches free to the patrons, especially undergraduate students seem to prefer database searches to searching in the printed indexes, not only because of the extensive searching capabilities, but because they end up with printed lists of citations.

# Chapter 3.
# Identification of Reference Sources

Reference sources in an academic library are noncirculating materials kept in separate reference locations and as smaller collections at a service desk. However, in reality, in addition to the reference collection, reference librarians consider the whole library collection as a source of information for persons they are assisting. Thus, in addition to being able to find information in the reference collections, reference librarians must be able to identify materials from the collection at large which may be useful for patrons.

Reference works can be defined by their function or attributes.[1] Some titles are included in the reference collection for administrative reasons, such as frequently used items or those prone to theft or mutilation.[2] Sometimes authoritative texts are kept at the desk. Bates' designation of reference works as sources which are "composed substantially or entirely of files"[3] seems a useful definition. This definition provides reference librarians with an easy criteria for assigning something to the reference collection.

The terms "sources" and "materials" are used instead of "reference books" because some reference-structured files are stored in computer databases accessed through online terminals or on CD-ROMs rather than in printed books or serials. Reference files may consist of data files such as the census files, bibliographic databases which contain citations to books and periodicals, or electronically produced books and journals in full text, such as the *Oxford English Dictionary* or the *Directory* of the American Library Association.

It is not the intention of this book to list actual reference titles. There are works which provide such lists with discussion and examples,[4] and others that simply list the most generally agreed upon reference sources for library school study or for reference collections.[5]

Because concepts for inquiries and categories relate directly to reference sources, librarians can readily choose sources. In fact, the ability of librarians to search reference sources efficiently is a major advantage for students requesting assistance with their information problems. Even when they are unaware of specific reference sources, librarians have the methodologies necessary to identify and evaluate them.

Reference librarians will choose which sources to suggest on the basis of their knowledge of sources, via use of library catalogs, or by using secondary reference works. From their library school education, librarians will have a thorough knowledge of types of reference sources with some examples of each type, but they will certainly not have learned the full range of sources available to them even in small reference collections. While it is important for them to know titles, they are much better served knowing the types that exist, how to find them and how to evaluate them for use.

Librarians identify sources through the library's catalog either by finding the call number for known reference titles or by identifying possible reference sources that do not immediately come to mind, making use of form divisions used with subject headings. The form divisions in the *Library of Congress Subject Heading List* are helpful in identifying sources, but are not foolproof because the form divisions have not been applied consistently.[6] Encyclopedias are included under the form "Dictionaries." In the case of periodical indexes there are several different kinds of headings used. Indexes to periodicals may be listed with the form subdivisions "Indexes," "Bibliographies" or "Catalogs." Also, if indexes cover a number of subjects, they are usually listed under one general heading which is not useful for the specific subjects included in the index.[7]

As the library profession has developed, librarians and publishers have prepared a number of secondary sources to help librarians identify reference sources. For the novice reference librarian particularly, they are very useful.[8] Major titles for reference librarians are guides to the literature of reference.[9] More recently the New York Public Library has published a general guide.[10] Similar to these are guides to the literature of a subject which include reference works. Librarians should know many of these sources or be able to identify them readily even though, like the periodical indexes, the subheadings are a problem. Guides to the literature are usually included under the subheading "bibliographies," which identifies many other types of bibliographies as well.

Other works have been developed to assist reference librarians in various areas: bibliographies of bibliography,[11] *Directories in Print*,[12] *Biography and Genealogy Master Index*,[13] *Gale Directory of Databases*.[14] These help the librarian identify which reference source to consult. It is these tools, designed to assist the librarian, which are most often found in ready reference collections.

Identifying the best index to periodicals for a student can be a complex search problem. The complexity is seen readily when a librarian teaches a library research class to identify indexes and abstracts.[15] Librarians suggest several alternatives: use of the library catalog, a guide to the literature of a subject, Ulrich's through specific periodical titles, and searching CALLS (California Academic Libraries List of Serials) on MELVYL.[16] For the class, librarians recommend that the students, after they try other techniques, query reference librarians or subject specialists as to which are the best of the identified indexes in terms of usefulness for students' topics. The students find that the same titles usually appear in the various sources, but they still have to select the index or abstract best for their topic. It is with this selection that reference librarians prove particularly helpful.

Librarians may solve the problem of identifying indexes by preparing materials to help. These may include a subject index to the library's indexes and abstracts or to its CD-ROMs, or mini-guides to the literature of a subject field. Commercial guides can be of help in a library as well. Online vendors provide printed catalogs of their databases by subject categories or databases such as DIALINDEX which give postings for all or selected databases.

## *Choice of Sources*

Once reference sources have been identified, the librarian has to decide which to recommend. Librarians will begin with the source which is most likely to contain the answer and be available, but will consider ease of use as a major factor if students will be searching the source themselves.

For example, before the issuance of *Sociological Abstracts* on a CD-ROM, the preferred recommendation for ease tended to be *Social Sciences Index* because it listed articles directly under subjects and subdivisions and had a format which students might be familiar with from having used the *Readers' Guide to Periodical Literature* sometime in the past. *Sociological Abstracts* used a two-step process and had general subject headings which might be difficult to use for specific topics. But in using the CD-ROM for *Sociological Abstracts*, students can now search words in the title or abstracts as well as the subject headings of the printed tool. Now since both sources are available in CD-ROM format, librarians will more likely base their recommendation on which will most likely provide articles for the information sought.

Tools that require use of microfilm or microfiche are less likely to be recommended or used. However, a librarian who enjoys the complexities of using the HRAF (Human Relations Area File)[17] and appreciates the kind of materials it contains might recommend it, making sure the student understands how to use it. In some cases, the HRAF may be the only possible source, for the alternative may be the book catalog of the Peabody Museum of Archaeology and Ethnology, which is almost as difficult to use because it uses local subject headings.

This brings up the time factor. Showing someone how to use the HRAF may take more time than the librarian should be away from the desk. Explaining the intricacies of using the *Social Sciences Citation Index* may also be time consuming. Ideally, librarians will recommend the best source and take the time to instruct the student in its use rather than merely select the quickest and easiest. The source to recommend is one of the decisions a librarian makes in assisting students.

# Chapter 4.

# Referral

The best strategy for some requests is to make a referral. Referrals are the means used by librarians to assist students if their informational needs are more readily met in another location or by another person within the library, within the library system, in a library outside the system or even in a non-library institution.[1]

Quality referral service in an academic library is recognized as an important element in the provision of superior reference service. Referral is listed as a standard in the 1979 document on information service[2] and in the 1991 guideline for medical, legal and business response.[3]

Authors who discuss failures in reference service note that not only do librarians give wrong answers, but they are even more likely not to make the referral which could provide the correct answer. McClure and Hernon have been particularly active in making assessments of reference service, especially in the area of government publications. Both in their book[4] and their article on referral in U.S. Depository Libraries,[5] they suggest that a number of the factors connected with the referral process be studied in order that referrals be improved and thus, service in general be improved.

Librarians may decide to make a referral at any time during the reference encounter based on what they discover about the request. They will refer students to someone else or to another collection of materials because the students' requests for assistance involve a subject, special skill, language or type of service which librarians can provide more expeditiously elsewhere. Librarians may decide to make a referral based on how efficiently help might be given in terms of the time and effort of the student or based on where the most recent information can be found if currency is important. A librarian may also refer a student if he has been unable to develop good rapport with the student or if he thinks perhaps two heads will be better than one in solving the student's informational problem.

Librarians may send students to another location simply for information or a specific source, but more often they refer students for assistance in the identification and use of information sources at that location. In some cases, the referral may take the form of a telephone call for information. If a librarian has determined that specific items are at another location, she may, instead of suggesting that the student go to the location, assist the student in obtaining the material via interlibrary loan or document delivery. Although perhaps obvious, it is worth stating that librarians send students to persons as well as places.

## *The Span of Referral*

As a freshman at a large university, the author's daughter was a bit shocked to discover when working on her first paper in the interdisciplinary subject of environmental sciences that her campus had 22 separate libraries. Since she had started her research at an undergraduate library, there were at least three other libraries if not more where she could find information on her topic. None of these was very close to the undergraduate library, although two were reasonably close to each other. While she partially obtained her referral to these libraries bibliographically through a union catalog, she equally could have been and probably was referred to the other libraries by librarians at the undergraduate library.

Multiple branch or divisional libraries are not unusual in large university library systems. These branches or divisions are usually staffed by librarians with a wealth of subject knowledge about their collections. These librarians are in a better position to assist the student with informational needs in their subject than the general reference librarian.

Even if a university does not have libraries spread out around a huge campus, it will undoubtedly have a large enough library system to have multiple service points for the needs of its students. While the problem of misdirection is not as severe in the single building library, misdirection in a building the length of two football fields and with 12 stack levels can be equally daunting as going to another library across the campus.

## Reasons for Referral

The shortage of funds for collections has forced libraries to become more specialized. No longer able to collect comprehensively, they now collect for their clientele. In order to obtain what their students need, libraries have worked collectively to define what they do collect in order to make possible the sharing of materials.

It is in this area of referrals outside the library system to other institutions that the most changes are occurring. Following the public library model, academic libraries have developed networks, first for exchange of materials and eventually for question referrals. In the public library model, questions are routinely sent to network centers for identification of the best source for the information, whether it be in a library or elsewhere. Questions may also be sent up the hierarchy from branch to central library, to regional information centers or to a state library center. These central units usually have larger collections.

Databases such as OCLC and RLIN already exist which can provide the basis for information request referral as they already provide for the exchange of materials. Electronic networks such as Internet provide for national and global information exchange. However, many requests are still sent through the mail. The Cooperative Reference Service Committee of the Reference and Adult Service Division of the American Library Association has developed a form which can be used for mail requests.[6] Low phone rates, fax machines and electronic mail make it increasingly possible, however, to refer a question to a distant location and receive an answer back within a feasible time framework.

Another built-in reason for referrals is the result of libraries putting materials in storage both locally and regionally. While retrieving materials can be fairly easy, using the stored materials to find information can be a problem. When a whole book truck load of a Russian periodical index needed to be searched, the whole run had to be sent for the user to search.[7] Systems will have to be devised for referral of inquiries to these locations so that the materials themselves do not always have to be sent. Perhaps in the above instance it would have been possible for the user to go to the storage facility.

As the information load for librarians increases, librarians have become more specialized in order to cope with the information explosion. With this specialization comes an increase in the opportunities and necessity for referrals.

While reference librarians may be paragons of all virtue, they cannot possibly know everything or even know how to locate information on all subjects; Kemp states, "It is not reasonable to think that every reference staff member will have the subject background and knowledge of sources to answer every question."[8] In fact, reference librarians probably can serve students better if they do not try to keep every possible bit of information in their memory banks. Thus, when the staff of a library is large enough, even without branch or divisional collections, it is useful for service to have subject specialists who are able to provide in-depth service in specialized subjects.

Subject specialization by librarians has become a growing trend, with graduate degrees in subject fields being required across the board by some institutions and for specific positions by others. Subject specialists, particularly those with foreign language facility, may work in other departments in the library (such as catalog or bibliographic searching), they may have joint appointments in reference and another department, or they may be in a branch library. Although there is some reluctance to refer students to non-reference librarians, a reference librarian should be willing to refer a student to the appropriate specialist wherever that person may be located in the library system.

Language specialists can be a great help to generalist librarians, both for speaking with foreign visitors and for translating foreign titles or phrases. Language expertise is essential in the more exotic areas of inquiry such as Islamic, Chinese or Russian subjects.

Even with Spanish, it can be helpful to have someone fluent available for librarians who can only make do with a dictionary or can only catch a word or two when spoken to.

Actually, specialization on the part of reference librarians may be just the result of one librarian having had more experience with particular resources than someone else. Examples of such resources might include the Human Relations Area File, the microfilms of early books listed in the Short Title Catalog or elsewhere, Newsbank indexes, the Chicano Data Base on CD-ROM or, for government publication librarians, census data or tax materials. Sometimes when the referral is to someone with greater expertise, referring librarians will follow along to learn from their colleagues so that perhaps the next time they will not have to make a referral.

When database searching was first instituted in a library, often only a few librarians performed searches because of the training required and the cost of that training. In such institutions, if an online search was determined to be useful, students were referred to a searcher. Later, as more librarians became searchers, librarians became adept at searching databases in the area of their expertise and received referrals for searches in these. Even when every reference librarian in a library is expected to be able to perform ready reference searches both online and via CD-ROM, referrals to subject specialists should still occur.

Perhaps it is more difficult for librarians to recognize the need for referral as a more efficient way of assisting the student. Most generalist librarians can search the databases for scientific subjects, but once they realize that they are bogged down by not understanding the specialized vocabulary or that it will take students more time, they know it is better to make a referral. Subject specialists with a more intimate knowledge of the sources in a given area or greater skill in searching databases in their field should not only be more efficient in providing service, but more able to satisfy students' in-depth subject needs.

Sometimes even though students' answers can be located in the general reference collection, students may be referred elsewhere because the source is more readily available there. Referral to locations for ease of use primarily applies to telephone requests.

The question of currency enters into the decision to refer as well. If a newspaper index or *Facts on File* is more apt to report who the most recently elected head of state in a nation is, it is foolish to send a person to Government Publications because information on leaders of countries is usually found there, but in sources not as current as those in the Reference Department.

Another occasion for a referral may arise if a particular librarian is too busy to handle the question or if he has such poor rapport with the student that another librarian could better assist the student. The referral in this case might depend on the availability of staff. This kind of referral can hardly be considered a routine matter, but service librarians should be aware that it may happen. Knowing students would receive better help from someone else, librarians should feel free to make this kind of referral, as well as any other, without guilt feelings.

While referring students because of subject is clear, in a library system there are also functional rather than subject service points to which students may be sent. Loan service desks provide for needs of students in obtaining materials for use at home. They determine checkout policy and procedures, provide for recalling and holding materials, levy overdue fines and provide information as to whether something is unavailable because it is checked out. Some online catalogs now provide circulation information. While reference librarians need to know basic circulation policies, staff members in other parts of the library need not necessarily know the policy on library cards or the fine schedule or handling a problem with a fine when the staff at the loan service desk are the experts.

Serials desks, as another example, handle requests for information on receipt or circulation of serial materials. Closely related to subject collections are format collections such as maps, microfilms or records and tapes, all of which are also destinations for referral.

Students sometimes request assistance in areas where it is inappropriate for librarians to assist students; for example, in choosing a doctor, seeking legal aid or solving a personal problem. Referrals in these cases should be made to the appropriate social agency.

## *When to Refer*

Librarians may decide to refer a student at any time during the reference transaction: in the interview, either immediately when the request is stated or after the exact nature of the question has been determined; in working out a search strategy; in demonstrating and assisting students with sources; or in ascertaining the success of the transaction.

When librarians first speak with students, they may immediately send students elsewhere recognizing that the materials for the subject are located elsewhere. This may occur, for example, if the subject is biological or if the question is political. Referring the student this quickly is not always a careful approach. By discussing the request for assistance, librarians may discover that the student would be better off using general reference materials for the biological subject because she wants material on a popular level or because the information wanted, although of a political nature, would not necessarily be contained in government publications.

Most referrals are made after the librarian thoroughly understands what the student is looking for. In the process of using an online union catalog, librarians may not only identify the existence of materials which answer the student's question, but may discover that materials for students are elsewhere in the library or the library system, or even in some other library system. This discovery may occur after citations from a CD-ROM database or a periodical index are found not to be owned by the library.

If specific works have been identified which are available at another location, librarians will be making what could be labeled bibliographic referrals. Students can be referred to the library where the materials are held or may acquire the material through interlibrary loan or document delivery. Librarians should explain the request procedure and help the students fill out the forms.

Besides not generally being offered to the undergraduate student, interlibrary loan may not be possible because of the expense or because the material does not circulate. Universities or colleges may charge non-affiliated users for searching, copying and mailing.

Since librarians verify with students the success of the search while the search is in process, they may receive further information about students' needs which indicates that they should make a referral rather than continuing the search. Negative results, partial answers or time consuming searches may also suggest referral to the librarian as she is working with the student.

Reference librarians are most comfortable making referrals to locations where they know specific sources exist. They feel successful having identified materials that can be obtained for students. Yet, in spite of the existence of effective interlibrary loan, there are times when graduate students, and faculty members as well, may need to use archives and special collections throughout the United States or Europe in pursuit of their research materials.

Finding materials for projects requiring use of primary materials, manuscripts and papers may be the joint responsibility of the library specialist and the faculty member.[9] For referrals to distant locations, the librarian and the faculty member should do everything possible to verify that the material actually is at that location and available. In some cases, the librarian will find it profitable to call or write the library, especially if there are indexes to specialized collections which can be consulted. These may be compiled at the distant location and available only at that site, as for example in the case of the biography file at the California State Library or the architecture file in the L.A. Public Library History Department.

## *Where to Refer*

Good referral is predicated on the knowledge the librarian has of the other unit or person or on the availability of files and directories which can be readily used to identify where to refer the student.

Some resources are already in existence for locating experts, and efforts have been made to provide resources on a more informal basis. Such tools might include standard reference sources such as the *Directory of Information and Referral Services in the United States and Canada, Subject Collections,* and the *Encyclopedia of Associations.*[10]

For in-house and some external referrals, manuals at the

reference desk will be the ideal location to keep information and materials needed for referral. The published brochures which the various branches or units of a library system have put out on their own collections, specialized materials, indexes or services should be included in a reference manual. For example, the location of sources for patents or for the documents listed in *American Statistics Index* should be in the manual.

Printed or typed materials are essential, but personal knowledge of the other units in a library system is even more useful for referring librarians. Librarians may obtain this knowledge in several ways. One department may acquaint another department with its sources. In Dunn and White's study of referral, such orientation to the collections of the other institutions proved to be the most valuable part of the Pomona-Covina Multitype Network project which they developed.[11] An exchange of personnel, with librarians from one institute or department actually working on the desk at another institution, is also useful.[12] This personal experience was the most valuable parts of the Pomona-Covina program, but the most difficult for them to implement because some librarians could not be released to work in another institution.[13]

Personal contact between librarians may be established through professional meetings or workshops of various types. Now, librarians can become acquainted through discussion groups over the Internet. These contacts may prove useful for referral purposes at a later time. Contacts of this nature can also be useful for librarians pursuing their own library studies.

## *Responsibilities for Making Referrals*

Competent librarians make referrals in such a way that students know that the librarians want the best for them and for that reason are directing them to someone who knows more in a given area. At any college or university, students should readily understand the nature of expertise and not think poorly of librarians who recommend they see someone else. Students also have to know that librarians are not just sloughing them off on someone else.

If the referral is directly to another person, the referring librarian can rephrase the student's question as he understands it, or if he sends the student elsewhere, he can explain to the student how to ask her question in terms of possible reference sources and to show the kind of information needed.

Telling the student to ask about specific sources may be useful, but it may also result in the other librarian's not being free to use her own expertise. The student told to ask for a specific source may ask directly for the source and never give the librarian the chance to find out exactly what the student needs, thus perhaps missing out on materials that would be more apt to produce results.

For example, a freshman student is told to use *Historical Abstracts* in print form for a short paper. The librarian may prefer to suggest using the *Humanities Index* because the student does not need the extensive coverage and the latter index will be easier to use. The availability of CD-ROMs for either index may very well change the recommendation.

While statistical questions may be referred routinely, say from General Reference to Government Publications[14] where the *American Statistics Index* on CD-ROM is located, the government publications librarian may be able to provide the information more easily from other sources.

It is useful for librarians to verify the success of referrals ahead of time by calling the desk to which a student is being sent. The librarian can explain the student's needs as she sees them and determine that the student will be helped there. Also, work on the question can be started while students are in transit. Calling ahead can keep referring librarians from feeling that they have sent students on a wild goose chase.

The only caution about librarians starting work on a question is the problem of students never arriving. Referring librarians should do everything possible to insure that the student actually arrives. Information may include the name of the person to ask for, the address of the facility, and the unit within it. Librarians should give careful and precise directions to the other location. Plans of the library or maps of the campus may be helpful.[15]

For certain kinds of questions when librarians know another

library has a specific source for information, librarians may simply call the other library for the information. If time is not a factor, librarians may write (or use fax or electronic mail as alternatives) the other library for the information or recommend that students write making sure students have the pertinent information to make their requests.[16]

If librarians work well together in a collegial atmosphere, referral can be on a much more casual basis, with librarians pooling their ideas on a good source. Logistics of this approach can be difficult if the librarians are very busy, but referral consultations can be very rewarding for the librarians. Contact with librarians beyond the local environment can widen the horizons of the referring librarian.

To mitigate the effects of possible poor service by the person to whom one refers a student, it is wise to ask the student to return if he has not been successful in finding what he needs. Thus, referring librarians indicate to students that they are not making the referral because they do not care, but because they do care and will continue to do so. However, the logistics of a return visit may be difficult if it is a ten or fifteen minute walk back to the referring librarian.

## Why Referrals Are Not Made

To a certain extent, referrals in academic and public libraries have followed different patterns because of the difference in goals of the two types of institutions. For small public libraries that are part of consortia or networks, librarians routinely refer questions to a bibliographic center or an information center.

It has been stated that public reference librarians generally serve their patrons by providing information, and college and university reference librarians primarily instruct.[17] While college reference librarians do not generally provide answers as such—that is, pieces of information—they do much more than instruct students. They assist in locating information which will serve for the completion of a student's assignment or in many cases as evidence to support the thesis of a student's paper. As such, what is found is not necessarily a specific piece of information or answer. Thus, the reference librarian can work out a number of alternate ways of finding information (i.e., evidence) for the undergraduate student which preclude referral.

Libraries in academic settings exist to support the academic program. Thus, librarians work with the students on their assignments so that students can find what sources and materials they need within the library rather than requesting materials through interlibrary loan. This, of course, is mainly true for the undergraduate student. Thus, librarians on a small campus will not refer students to another campus unless the situation is hopeless. They will do everything possible to help the student find something in their own library. In general, librarians are reluctant to make referrals.

However, if students are unsuccessful and have not been referred, they may seek out other campuses or agencies on their own, learning of them through friends and colleagues. If they decide they have to have one specific item, they will request it on interlibrary loan where this is possible on their campus.

In not making a referral, librarians to some extent are telling students that it is not worth their energy, time or money to go somewhere else. However, librarians should present the information about sources at other libraries and the problems connected with going to other locations so that students can decide for themselves.

Lack of referrals or poor referrals may be the result of personal characteristics of the librarian. Good referrals are a regular function of good reference service. The bottom line for good reference service is the librarian who really wishes to help the student.

Librarians may fail to make referrals because of lack of self-knowledge and self-confidence. A librarian who is possessive about a question and feels it is his responsibility to answer it may be unwilling to refer the question to someone else even if he knows that it may take him longer or that he may not be providing a desirable level of service. Librarians may be insecure about their ability to help students. If librarians are anxious about students' attitude towards them, if they worry students may think they are stupid when they admit they do not know something, they may not make a referral which would benefit students.

Also of little help are librarians who assist a student without realizing that they do not know the best source or approach, and thus do not recognize that a referral should be made. This is an especially acute problem with referrals by student assistants and library paraprofessionals who want to help students, but do not recognize their own limitations. Like librarians, they may not want to make a referral for the same reasons, but unless they have outstanding training, they may never negotiate the question to the point that they realize the student would be better off if they made a referral.

It is easy to see how experienced librarians may worry that the expert will not give students the same tender loving care they give or that even though other librarians have the subject expertise, they might not handle the question any better than referring librarians could. A certain amount of faith and trust in fellow librarians is necessary. Recognition that librarians have their own individual styles of handling questions helps in letting go of a question.

## *Feedback*

Most librarians want some sort of feedback on their referrals. Since one of the features of a successful reference transaction is the verification that students have received the help they need,[18] librarians will wish to know students' success at the referred location. This can be done informally by librarians asking the person who received the referral the next time they see the person or making a point of asking for the results of the referral from them at a later time. It can be accomplished through a system of forms that can be returned to the person making the referral. It was found in two studies that librarians did not always take the time to fill out the forms or to return them, but that when they did, the information was valuable to the persons making the referral.[19] The form appears to be a useful idea, but without a great deal of incentive, it is impractical because forms are either not filled out or not returned to the referring librarian because of time factors.[20]

Sometimes librarians are reluctant either to give away their trade secrets or to have another librarian be in a position to judge the validity of how they have answered the question when asked for feedback. In a collegially organized department, these concerns are inappropriate if not in violation of professional ethics. Yet the request for feedback means that librarians care enough about their service to wish to improve their referrals in the future or their knowledge of sources in general.

It should be a goal of librarians to develop the kind of procedures and support to make meaningful referrals and to develop the personal skills to identify the need, the ability to assure the student, and the willingness to insure that students find the person or place where they can have their information needs satisfied.

# Chapter 5.

# Making Use of Sources

Reference librarians have a responsibility for the use of the sources that they provide. They can turn students loose to use them with the suggestion that the students return for more help if they cannot find what they want, or they can go with the students to the source. In the case of a one-volume work, librarians can ask students to bring the volume to the desk if they need assistance with it.

From experience, reference librarians will usually know how to use a tool. If they do not, they can figure out how to use the tool more quickly than the student by scanning the preface and introduction or initial explanatory information to determine how to use the tool and what the symbols used may stand for. Librarians can recommend that students read the explanatory material themselves.

By searching the source with or for the student, they can verify the student's success in finding information immediately and know whether further explanation is needed for searching. The recognition of understanding by the student is insured by asking the question, "Does this completely answer your question?" Use of this question appears to be the single most important part of the reference encounter, as it can improve service to students by insuring that the correct answer is obtained.[1]

If several sources have been recommended, librarians will either have to show each of them to the student or ask the student to return if the first source has not been of any use. Undergraduate students in particular find it confusing to have several sources suggested. They would prefer to have librarians suggest the best source rather than be left to determine this on their own. But students may learn more about problem solving in the library if they have to look at several sources before determining which to search first.

Librarians should explain to students the arrangement of entries in a reference work, the use of abbreviations or symbols and the types of indexes provided. The specificity of the index is important. Most people have encountered indexes that use general terms with many page numbers given. These indexes would be more useful if broken down into more specific subjects. For some periodical indexes, thesauri are provided which list more specific headings, broader headings or related headings. Use of a thesaurus can improve a subject search.

Librarians often help students who come to the desk because they have not had success in their searches. When students do not find information on their own or do not find the materials they need, librarians should help students look. Librarians will need to solve problems for the student or suggest alternate books on the same subject by using the subject headings that described the original book. They may suggest the use of interlibrary loan, if available, to secure the work cited after determining that the book is in another library which will lend the book to the student.

Discussing how to help students use sources brings up the question of how much service to give the student. The extent of service and how it shall be offered to students has been discussed in the literature for some time. Some librarians advocate one kind of service, while others prefer other kinds: conservative, liberal, find the answer, instruct the student, direct the student, assist the student, or any combination of these.[2] Lynch states this as a question, "Do we find information or show others how to find it?"[3] Even if available, guidelines cannot be followed rigidly as if they were cast in concrete. Yet the reference department should define an ideal level of service in a set of guidelines in the reference policy manual.

Librarians, because they are professionals, will have to judge the extent of service they give on the basis of time available, nature of the question, and needs of the student within the guidelines of the policy statements. Actually, the type of service which reference librarians give may also be the result of the personal styles of librarians which have been developed over time through their experiences in helping students.

It would be nice to use the dictum "never just point" to define an undesirable level of service in working with a student,[4] but in fact a simple question of location in the library may effectively be answered just that way. Indicating the location of materials in a reference section by call number or by the number of the table is justifiable, particularly for those students who might be incensed if the librarian suggested they needed more help. If librarians have pointed or indicated by call number or table number, whenever possible, they should follow up to make sure students have successfully located the source and used it to locate the information they need. Librarians should always ask students to return if they have not been completely successful.

With catalogs and indexes in many forms available online at the reference librarian's service counter, the initial research that often follows the reference interview can be started at the desk, but if it starts at the desk it should not necessarily end there. It is difficult for reference librarians to assist students without being on their feet, even at a desk. At a desk of counter height, the librarian will most likely be standing, and at a low desk she will stand to greet the student so that she will be at the student's level. It seems that reference librarians are always on their feet assisting students. In listing the physical attributes for librarians of energy, tirelessness and stamina, Thomas speaks of having "marvelous feet."[5] The fact is that students respond better to librarians who actively pursue assisting them.

Of course, when working with a student side by side, it is appropriate for both to be seated, as for example when helping with *Social Sciences Citation Index*, which has small type and is difficult to read from a standing position. Working at the same level fosters a sense of cooperative partnership in solving a problem.

Librarians and students expect that students will do their own work, both because they wish to be independent and because they are expected to learn how to use the library as part of their college education.[6] The assumption is that they will request help in using the library and in learning to use the library when they need it. As

Whitlatch states, "The role of the academic reference librarian should be to empower users to serve themselves."[7]

In a successful reference encounter, the librarian will not go zip-zip-zip and provide answers, but will verbalize what he is doing as he goes along so that the lesson is in the explanation if the student wishes to learn it: find the access tool (catalog or serials list), obtain the call number, locate call number in the library, find material on the shelf (shelves, special areas, storage).

Librarians should explain the process in working with students—for example, in using an online catalog, reference source, indexes to periodicals or CD-ROMs—if for no other reason than to verify that the source recommended has the information needed. Librarians will save students a great deal of frustration by helping them identify sources and showing them how to use them. Choice of subject headings is a major problem solving area in the search for information. Understanding the citations in order to find the material in the library is a less annoying problem, but may require assistance.

When librarians know information on a subject is difficult to access even in available sources or when sources are difficult to use, they should work with the student, at least until the librarian is confident the student can manage on her own. The ease of use of a reference tool and type of information being sought are criteria which regulate the degree of help the librarian offers.

For example, when the students are looking for an association, librarians can simply hand them the index to the *Encyclopedia of Associations* and leave them to proceed on their own, or if time is available, they can actually find the association in the index and find the listing in the right volume more readily before explaining the information given.[8] Some librarians would consider this spoon-feeding the student. Another instance would be the identification of an index to use for a subject making use of Ulrich's periodical directory. The librarian can do the search by title of the periodical and then explain how indexes to periodicals are listed, interpreting the abbreviations and making a recommendation on which index would best serve the subject request.

The provision of periodical indexes in CD-ROM format can be

another example for the discussion of the extent of service given. To a degree, use of materials on CD-ROMs is self service. Students often select the databases and do their own searches without the assistance of librarians, perhaps making use of leaflets.

This service has only provided access to the database. More extensive service might be helpful for inexperienced students. Librarians can suggest databases, and after students obtain them, librarians can demonstrate accessing them and explain the protocols and kinds of subject headings which can be used (including comments on when a thesaurus might be helpful). The most extensive service is for librarians to do, or at least begin the actual search for the student. Actually, mediated online computer searches are examples of this extensive service.

While students are supposed to find CD-ROMs user friendly, they may misunderstand what is included in the database or how to construct a search strategy. Inexperienced students thinking in terms of their topic rather than the structure of the database may request such a detailed list of subjects that they will have no results, or they may request such a general topic that the large number of articles retrieved is daunting and includes many articles useless for their topics. If the suggestion is made to students that they ask librarians for assistance either before they begin or when the results are not what they hoped for, fewer students will sit in frustration in front of terminals. A roving librarian can be particularly useful in watching out for students in trouble with their searches on CD-ROMs and with an online catalog as well.

A recent study was made of end-user searches compared with experienced librarian searches on the ERIC database. The study concluded that the end-users did well on precision but that they "miss many items that they later judged useful. More importantly, they missed many of the items that they judged particularly important."[9] The conclusion expressed reservations about end-user searches: "A greater danger lies in the fact that they give some library users a false sense of security—the feeling that because the source is 'technological,' they are finding everything or, at least, finding the best materials."[10] Solutions were offered in the report of the study: instruction, search tools to aid the user, or sophisticated interfaces.

Besides general indications of extent of service for desk service, the policy guidelines for service should include watching out for users in trouble either from the desk, while walking through the reference area, or by peeking over the shoulders of those using computer terminals. Students may well ask for assistance from librarians on the move in their area when they would not approach a desk. It is better to err on the side of being pushy in offering service rather than being too reticent.

Reference librarians explain the shelving system to students and help them identify where they may have gone wrong in their search for an item on the shelves. Possibilities include the materials' being in a special location or students' not understanding the decimal nature of part of the call number. Reference librarians make suggestions for finding books when the student has been unable to locate the material, such as checking circulation status, considering logical misfilings, looking on tables near the shelves, looking on shelves where books are placed for reshelving or checking the trucks with books ready for reshelving.

Although reference librarians find it difficult to leave the desk except for short periods of time, they sometimes feel that it is important to go to the shelves with users. Not only does this present a wonderful opportunity to teach users how to find materials in the library, but it may inform librarians of peculiarities of the shelving system which are new or which they were unaware of. With this information, librarians can help the next person with the same problem.

## Instruction at the Desk

Librarians will not wish to bore or insult students with instruction on the use of something the students already know how to use. On the other hand, students may be put off if librarians give their solution to the problem without adequately demonstrating how to go from "I need" to "Does this look like it will answer your question?"

Although already implied in the discussion on extent of service, whether reference librarians should be instructors on the desk is another policy decision. Nevertheless, the library director must project to the academic faculty the meaning of the librarian's teaching role. Professors should be encouraged to refer students to the reference staff. There seems to be no question that in a college or university setting, librarians should take every opportunity to instruct the students they assist.

Howell et al. report that "The university library clientele, which is habituated to teacher-student role relationships, responds unusually favorably to the librarian as teacher."[11] Librarians will be negligent if they miss the opportunity to teach students in the process of assisting them to find what they need. The students may not recognize that there is a lesson being taught, but they are generally more satisfied with the encounter if instruction occurs.[12]

When librarians encounter advanced students, it is imperative that they share their knowledge of specific tools in the students' field of concentration. Librarians have discovered Ph.D. candidates who lamented not learning of some specialized tools earlier in their career. With greater emphasis placed on bibliographic instruction at the present time, perhaps this is less apt to occur. Librarians as teachers will be discussed more thoroughly in the section on library instruction later, but it is obvious that part of a reference transaction must be instruction.

From the librarians' point of view, they may wish to instruct students so that they will not have to help students with that particular kind of question again. What comes to mind as examples of repetitive questions are the steps which the student must use to locate a known book or periodical in the library. It is the recurrence of repetitive questions that suggests to librarians that a leaflet or expert system might be useful or that a paraprofessional at an information desk might just as easily assist the student.

A well prepared leaflet can often be given to students when they might have to wait for assistance otherwise. It can give in-hand instructions for them to see rather than listen to, particularly when they may need titles to search or protocols to use. Students using a leaflet can take responsibility for their own learning and will be in a better position to request the assistance which they really need.

The challenge of reference work in an academic library is for librarians to decide on the best way to assist every student, whether with minimum service, liberal service, instruction or whatever other means are appropriate. As Robinson states it, "Reference librarians are paid to exercise professional judgment and to make conscious choices when handling reference questions."[13]

## Chapter 6.

# End of the Transaction

Either librarians or students can terminate transactions. Reference transactions end when librarians sense or ask whether the student is satisfied with the assistance. As has been mentioned, the best conclusion is the question about whether the student's question has been completely satisfied.

Students may end transactions when they feel that they can proceed on their own, when they run out of time, or even because they are not finding the encounter satisfactory for any number of reasons. Even too much information or help can cause a student to back away from the transaction. Nolan suggests that librarians end transactions for knowledge-related factors, for communication reasons or for policy reasons.[1]

Some of the factors for transactions being concluded are not under the control of the librarians. There are too many students waiting to be helped; the library does not own the tool; policies prevent the librarian from assisting the student.[2]

Librarians will undoubtedly make some evaluation of how well a reference encounter has gone and how satisfied the student has been at its end. This evaluation may be immediate or retrospective and may include verification with another librarian about alternative search strategies and sources. At times, reference librarians may be so caught up with a request for information that they do not end their pursuit of information even after the student leaves and can no longer be given the information. In these cases, the librarian will either have asked the student to return or will hope he does. The librarian will learn from the search in order to apply this experience to inquiries in the future.

Reviewing the transaction is the librarian's last step in the reference encounter. For the reference department, the last step will be the evaluation of the success of encounters in general to identify the effectiveness of the department or the areas in which the department or individual librarian may need improvement.

It may not be possible for the librarian to know the success of the student's search because the student may only discover the usefulness of her materials when she is working with them at home or when her paper receives a high grade. Even if librarians cannot determine the "success" of the transaction, they usually have a grasp of whether students are satisfied with the assistance. It is not unknown for students, the next time they see the librarian, to comment on how helpful were the materials which were found.

## Chapter 7.

# Patron Contact Away from the Desk

In addition to the time spent assisting students at a desk, reference librarians also assist students away from the desk. It is not always possible for a librarian to say to the person taking over the desk when the clock strikes the hour, "This student is looking for an article on.... Would you show him...?" For example, this approach would not be appropriate if a student needed to use the *Performing Arts Index*, which requires a bit more explaining and help in the location of the file and how to search it than some sources. The student may think he is being shunted off, and in a way he is.

The librarian coming on duty will not have learned firsthand through talking with the student what the student wants and may feel it necessary to request more information to insure that the best strategy has been worked out to satisfy the student's need. This is laborious, or at least time consuming, for the student. It also may be a bit time consuming for the librarian leaving the desk to explain to the person taking over what she perceives as the student's need.

It is obviously better that the librarian finish the explanation and demonstration before going off duty. The effect of this added time indicates to the student that the librarian cares about his problems. However, when the librarian does leave the student, she should suggest that the student return to the desk and her colleague if the student has further problems.

But, even if the desk has highest priority, sometimes because of prior commitments it is impossible for a librarian to stay and complete a student's query. Then, the librarian has no other recourse than to turn the inquiry over to the replacing librarian. If she handles the situation with tact, she will retain rapport with the student for the department. However, if the librarian on the desk anticipates that there will not be time to assist the student fully, it is appropriate for her to ask the student to wait the few minutes necessary for the next librarian to appear.

Another scenario requiring a librarian to spend time assisting a student on reference questions off the desk is a telephone request. For example, there are three students and a faculty member waiting for assistance, and the phone rings. Unless someone else is assigned to take messages, the proper response is to answer the phone and place the student on hold or to take down the information and phone number promising to call the student back later.

If there continue to be lots of requests for help on the desk, it will not be possible for the librarian to return the call before going off duty. The librarian's colleague who comes on the desk also will clearly be too busy to work on the request for information. The librarian going off duty will need to work on the telephone request away from her desk duty. In many cases it is easier for the librarian to work on telephone requests when not assigned to the desk than when on desk duty, since there is less chance of interruptions or the appearance of ignoring waiting students.

Similarly, a librarian may negotiate requests for information with a student and discover that the only way she can assist the student is to work on the informational need when she is not on desk duty. In these cases, the librarian can request that the student come back at a later time when the librarian can devote more time to the question, or the librarian may locate the information while off the desk without the student. The librarian can set a time for the student's return for the information or leave the information at the desk to be picked up. If the librarian will be difficult for the student to find on the return visits, leaving the information at the desk may be the only option. Of course, librarians can also phone the student at a specified time or e-mail the information to the student.

Students may look for a favorite librarian for assistance because they have developed great rapport with that librarian and will receive the kind of help they like. The student may seek the librarian because of the librarian's subject knowledge, skill in locating information, or personal qualities such as warmth or display of interest. Obviously, librarians will assist those students when they are approached when not on desk duty if at all possible, whether the patrons are faculty members, graduate students, undergraduates or others.

## Database Searching

When a librarian is discussing possible sources with a students, she may conclude that the best way to assist the student is to do an in-depth computer search. Because the search will require further discussion to work out which databases to use and the best strategy to follow (search terms), the librarian will make an appointment with the student to return when the librarian is not assigned to the desk and can concentrate and take the time to search the database. While it is possible for students to request a database search and have it performed immediately by a librarian, most mediated online searches are accomplished by appointment.

A similar instance of off-desk reference is when a colleague introduces a specialist librarian, who is not on desk duty, to a student whose question is in the realm of the librarian's expertise and can most expeditiously be solved by the specialist. The specialist has two options, to drop what he is doing or to ask the student to return. If students are referred to librarians because of their expertise while they are off the desk, it is a judgment call. The decision on whether to drop everything and work with the student should be made on the basis of other commitments and time constraints. Unless the specialist has urgent commitments, it is best to help the student immediately rather than suggest that the student return.

The dilemma of dropping a current task to help a student may confront librarians at other times. Consider the following example: A librarian is seated at a CD-ROM station searching for professional literature on a library problem. A student at the next station is having difficulty and asks for help or indicates in some way that help might be useful. Does the librarian flash a "not assigned to the desk" button at the student and tell him to walk clear across the room to the librarian on duty, who is helping another student while a third student is waiting?

## Reference by Appointment

At the present time, it is thought that reference by appointment is a good way to assist students with in-depth research problems. Those who argue for reference by appointment insist that it makes sense for highly trained subject specialists or even generalists to work with the student on appointment, leaving the routine locational questions to be answered at a desk by paraprofessionals, students or expert systems. Reference by appointment makes it possible for librarians to be more effective in assisting students because they can do some preliminary work on the research problem before meeting with the students, and they can spend more time with students to insure that their informational needs are fulfilled.

Whether to close the reference desk and provide reference by appointment only is another question altogether which has been argued in the literature.[1] The profession feels that acting as a specialist in finding information is the proper role for the reference librarian.

Time and convenience are important factors with appointments. Students with extensive searches will be willing to return. But when in general only six minutes' time or less is spent on a reference question, it doesn't seem necessary or feasible to ask the student to return for assistance. Of course, if the student does return, he is likely to have the librarian spend more time in assisting him than the six minutes.[2] More time does not necessarily guarantee better service.

Reference by appointment can be informally handled, with librarians making their own appointments, but it is probably better to design a special program through which appointments are encouraged. Reference service by appointment can be advertised as a separate service or as part of term paper or thesis assistance,[3] or can be introduced at term paper clinics.

A procedure or mechanism for requesting and scheduling appointments should be set up. Forms which provide room for an explanation of the nature of the request may be used. Perhaps the departmental secretary can assist with the appointment program, or librarians may wish to speak with clients to make the appointment in order to have enough information to prepare for the session. Whatever the mechanism, it should be easy to follow and should provide the possibility of keeping numerical records of appointments.

## Roving Librarian

Librarians at a reference desk have always done some roving of reference areas, if only with their eyes. In large libraries with a spread-out collection and electronic equipment, it makes sense to assign a reference librarian or assistant to circulate, assisting students as they appear to be having difficulties. Students are often willing to request help from a librarian at hand when they would be reluctant to seek help at a desk.

Particularly at electronic work stations, rovers can offer students more basic reference help, conducting reference interviews and answering reference questions, as well as instructing on the use of the electronic facilities. Since they do not have students waiting to be helped, they can feel less rushed in providing in-depth help than they would if serving at a desk. A desk specifically designated for assistance with electronic facilities can be provided with the stipulation that the person at the desk watch out for problems and go with the student to the terminal.[4]

Providing a roving librarians may be difficult because of staffing problems; indeed, it may be possible only where there are interns or library school students available. It is another possibility for reference librarians to consider when they discuss restructuring reference service.

Ideally, for decisions on some of the instances discussed above, the reference department will have a policy statement to give librarians some direction as to when to give off-desk service. If there is no policy statement, librarians will have to make an individual judgment on how best to serve the student.

# PART II.

# Support for the Desk

This section includes diverse elements which are linked in that they, in some measure, support the work of the reference librarian on desk duty. Perhaps the best support for librarians has been to split the questions into levels by having paraprofessionals answer directional questions and provide simple explanations of computer use for searching through secondary desks. Computer facilities as support for the desk have provided better search tools as well as possibilities for searching in the whole world of bibliographic sources. They can also provide service through expert systems and the availability of e-mail service for telephone requests.

A librarian's basic knowledge of the collections and methods of searching is the foundation for good service. However, because new works are constantly produced and new search tools and methods developed, keeping current in knowledge is an ongoing process at which every librarian must work. For both new and experienced librarians, reference and information manuals can provide backup information which can be quickly looked up while assisting a patron.

*Chapter 8.*

# Alternate Provisions
# for Service

The provision of alternative methods of assisting patrons includes information desks as well as a reference desk (or even instead of a reference desk), expert systems,[1] or telephone calls received on information lines or by electronic means. These alternate provisions for service make it possible for reference librarians to concentrate on the kind of assistance which they are uniquely trained to give. By providing information desks, expert systems, or electronic telephone answering systems, personal assistance is split into levels of service which make a statement about staffing for these levels. These levels are considered part of tiered systems.[2]

## *Information Desks*

Information desks and catalog assistance desks of various kinds have been around for a long time as support for the reference desk. Information desks have provided answers to locational and informational questions, but they more recently have provided catalog assistance to students in the identification of materials in the catalogs and online facilities.[3] Even simple factual questions can be answered at an information desk provided the sources are available. Information desks are particularly useful in making referrals, not just to the reference desk, but to the person best able to assist the student. Expert systems and electronic means of helping the patron outside the library have been added more recently to support direct service to patrons. Electronic fielding of telephone calls is just beginning to gain acceptance.

Splitting personal assistance into levels of service makes better use of personnel in a time of either shrinking numbers of librarians or increased demands on librarians.[4] Library administrators save money by staffing information desks with library assistants or students. It is awkward for library administrators to make decisions on the basis of budgetary restraints, but in the case of library assistants at information desks, they may decide this is the best use of personnel.

Libraries have traditionally staffed information desks with paraprofessionals. Paraprofessionals are staff members who are not librarians, but the term does not include staff members who have clerical assignments in a library.[5] Usually paraprofessionals are library assistants who have better educations or more library experience than clerical personnel. Even though staffed with paraprofessionals, information desks may be supervised by librarians either directly or through library assistant supervisors.

A library may find it difficult to staff the information desk with library assistants since there may be staff shortages in all areas of the library. But if technical processing divisions are reorganized or service units combined, for example, there may be personnel free to be assigned to a desk. Also, with the recognition that injuries occur when staff members are required to sit at a terminal eight hours a day, these staff members may be relieved of terminal work by being assigned to an information desk.

Although probably not a usual solution, it may be a good idea for top library administrators to regularly spend an hour or two on the desk to keep their hands on the pulse of students' inquiries. They might also serve on a reference desk for the same reason. Their service on a reference desk would make it possible for all reference librarians to attend departmental meetings.

The decision to use paraprofessionals and students may affect the quality and quantity of service.[6] Some librarians have felt that paraprofessionals are not as successful in assisting the users because they fail to negotiate questions, fail to make referrals, and do not have sufficient knowledge of tools.[7]

With careful training and supervision, library assistants can indeed provide adequate service for questions about library service locations, ownership of materials and using online catalogs, and they can refer students for informational needs of a more specialized nature.[8]

To provide the quality of service, some librarians feel it is important for the student to encounter the highly trained professional first because the professional can more readily determine the nature of the request and insure that the student receives good service. A couple of examples: The student asks "Where are the encyclopedias?" when the information needed is the current leader of Mozambique. The student asks, "Where is the *Readers Guide?*" when the information needed is something on yellow-dog contracts. The professional librarian has greater facility in determining the information need behind the request for a specific tool. When library assistants field this type of question they can always invite the student to consult the reference librarian if they have been unsuccessful.

Another argument against the use of paraprofessionals is the blurring of roles which can occur. Students may become confused as to who is a librarian and who is a library assistant and what exactly a librarian does that is different. Unfortunately, students have always had this confusion. Even faculty members, when they have found library assistants particularly helpful, have become confused. Differentiation of staff between an information desk and a reference desk can help alleviate this problem of discernment. Librarians can indicate that they are indeed professionals through their more thorough assistance and their other provisions for service that indicate that they are equals with the faculty in the education of students.

Use of paraprofessionals is always predicated on adequate training. In giving this training, are librarians saying that what is learned in library school can be learned on the job? With fewer and fewer library schools in existence, will librarians need to be recruited and trained on the job just as library assistants are trained for work at information desks?

Library assistants can become angry when they perceive that

they are doing the same work as librarians and in many cases for less pay, although the salaries of many high level paraprofessionals do overlap those of beginning librarians. Library assistants usually compare themselves with librarians who have avoided the responsibilities of being a professional librarian by filling their time with routine tasks.

It is difficult for library assistants to understand that librarians have responsibilities assigned to them and are expected to work out their own methods of fulfilling them rather than having tasks assigned.[9] In fact, working together, reference librarians set goals and design the programs they are responsible for. Librarians determine what needs to be done and how to do it. Faculty or academic status for librarians requires them to operate as partners with the faculty in developing programs and organizing the library for service to the academic program.

The use of information desks and tiered service will not be eliminated in the near future, but will undoubtedly increase as librarians redefine what it means to be a reference librarian. Most library administrators, even if they are not certain that the advantages outweigh the disadvantages, will keep information desks as practical solutions to providing service.

## Expert Systems

Although they have not been universally adopted, expert systems can be part of a department's configuration for service. Expert systems consist of facts stored in a computer and programs which provide access to these facts. They offer support for reference service by assisting students when no librarian is scheduled or in answering locational, informational, and factual questions at any time.[10] Expert systems make it possible for librarians to share their expertise as the computer takes over many routine questions for the students.[11]

The interactive computer programs of expert systems ask users a series of questions that can be answered yes or no or by selecting responses from a menu of choices. On the basis of the answers, the program searches the database for recommendations to present to users. Programs are designed so that if certain facts are true, certain sources can be recommended. For example, if the answers to a series of questions asked indicate that information on an American biologist is sought, the current edition of *American Men and Women of Science* might be recommended.

Expert systems are written in programming languages such as LISP or PROLOG or even PASCAL or dBaseIII. Some systems have been developed using what are called shells which make the development of the system somewhat easier.[12] However, most librarians will need the help of "knowledge engineers" to develop a system.[13] One system has been developed that can be used for training librarians as well as serving as an expert system for students.[14]

Arguments against the installation of expert systems include the possible confusion of users as to which terminal to use among the proliferating computer terminals in libraries, or the possibility that the wiring of the building would be inadequate in an older library. The wiring problem may already have been addressed when other computer terminals were installed. Because expert systems are time consuming to develop (and thus expensive), an individual reference department may not have the time or funds available to develop them. However, as with instructional programs, existing programs can sometimes be adapted for the local library situation.

Many of the online facilities are similar to expert systems in assisting the student in their use. The help screens, often developed by reference librarians, lead students in making use of the information by giving them menu choices and access to help screens. It is reference librarians who will have to keep up to date on what information is in the database and how to gain access to it.[15] The design of student interfaces for online databases is a new area of responsibility for the reference librarian.

## Telephone

A reference department has to decide whether telephone service is important to its service. If the line is always busy or the caller must often be put on hold or the librarian cannot immediately or shortly call back on questions taken, the number of calls will decrease and a valuable service is not really being offered. Telephone service at the reference desk is practically impossible because of the many students seeking help within the library.

If telephone service is deemed important and considered a high priority, how to offer it needs to be worked out.[16] For example, one person could be assigned to answer telephone reference questions, perhaps at stated times. An information line answered by paraprofessionals can save numerous interruptions at a reference desk. The reference phone can either be hooked up to the information line for call referrals or be a separate line, or both options could be available. Messages can be taken on the information line rather than calls being transferred to reference.

Ready reference has been made available in a few libraries through a network making use of electronic mail facilities.[17] The questions are fielded via a computer. The answers are worked out by reference librarians and posted to the computer for availability through the network within a specific length of time.

Some libraries have made use of voice mail, accommodating multiple callers with multiple storage units for requests.[18] To be effective, the message which answers the caller when the phone is answered must be carefully worded, instructing callers to leave their phone number and to request a time to return the call.

The library's response to voice or e-mail requests needs to be timely. The reference department will have to develop a way of answering the requests, either assigning one person or parceling out the requests. Since the library's operating hours are one of the often asked questions, calls for voice mail can be switched to a line offering the hours.

Most patrons would probably prefer to have their request for information be taken by voice or e-mail rather than having have no telephone or very little telephone service offered.

*Chapter 9.*

# Preparation
# for the Desk

In order to be effective, reference librarians must put in some time off the desk to insure that they know the collection and the services offered by the library.

Knowing the collection will require an ongoing review of the collection and keeping up to date on what is being added to the reference collection. If the librarians are subject specialists, this knowledge will apply to additions to the collection in their particular subject areas as well.

Knowledge of the reference collection is a major requirement for reference librarians. While in a small library it may be possible to remember every book in a reference collection, in a large library this is impossible. It is probably not possible, particularly in the sciences, to know even the titles of every single index or abstract journal.

Yet, even in a large library, reference librarians must know the basic core of the collection,[1] the types of materials collected and in what languages, and will need a working knowledge of the most common types of access to them. Most important the librarian will need to be able to locate the bibliographic information and location of individual titles and where they are located, using either the library catalogs or secondary sources such as a guide to the literature of a subject.

Librarians have developed various ways of coping with the problem of identifying reference materials. They have developed elaborate subject files of all types of reference materials or just of indexes and abstracts (cards, notebooks, or computer produced lists). They have produced keyword indexes which can be used by librarians, faculty and students.[2] If the keyword index is produced by computer, it can also be mounted on the local online catalog for referral.[3] Reference librarians can more readily identify reference materials in online catalogs with keyword searching. Reference librarians have also produced guides to the literature of a subject which help both students and librarians. Although librarians identify titles through these access tools, the librarian will still have to make a judgment as to which to recommend. The judgment will be made on knowledge of the work, its date, publisher, indexing and scope.

Here are some examples of choices. A student needs information on the work of a Chicano writer and has found nothing directly in the subject catalog. Should the CD-ROM index to Chicano materials be recommended, or should it be the MLA bibliography on CD-ROM, the print indexes to *Contemporary Literary Criticism*[4] or *Twentieth-Century Literary Criticism*[5] or the *Dictionary of Literary Biography*[6] or even *Contemporary Authors*, or one of the master indexes to biographical sources? Since some of these choices are based on shots in the dark and might be time consuming to search, librarians are more apt to recommend the CD-ROM indexes. If the writer is somewhat obscure, librarians will need to follow up with students and perhaps assist them in the second or third choices if the first ones recommended have not netted pertinent articles.

For the new librarian, knowledge of the collection may require a scanning of the collection title by title with a closer look at unfamiliar types or titles over several weeks—no small task for librarians in academic libraries with collections in the thousands of titles. All reference librarians will have to review the new titles being added and take part in refresher workshops.

They may be assisted in learning new titles by an annotated in-house publication of new reference titles. The list of new titles is no substitute for examining the books, but it can be helpful for retrieval. If such a list is produced, one librarian will have to examine the books more thoroughly in order to prepare the new title list and annotations. Displaying new materials at the desk will assist librarians who can review new titles at slack times at the desk.

Reference librarians will have to have a working knowledge of the total collection and its idiosyncrasies, and of services offered by the library. Only by knowing this information can librarians lead orientation tours or make sensible referrals. Librarians should never assume that the library does not own a requested title or provide a service that is needed. Sufficient for reference librarians perhaps, in highly specialized requests, is a knowledge of where to find information on the collection and services throughout the library and other units.

Another activity useful for maintaining preparedness is keeping up with and practicing searches on electronic databases. This may require reading the serial publications of the online vendors to learn of new databases or innovations in searching. Keeping current in online searching may also require attendance at vendor-sponsored workshops.

Most libraries will put out news about online catalog changes, additions and development. This is probably the best way to inform the user of what is happening to the database because the information is available for anyone using the online catalog. One online union catalog (UC MELVYL) not only provides news and information online, but has an experimental mode in which innovations are tried out to elicit feedback before they are incorporated into the main system.

In-house training sessions are a good solution for introducing or keeping librarians up to date or reminded of collections, services, methodologies, resources, online and CD-ROM searching techniques and discussions of problem solving stratagems. There are enough topics to cover that these training sessions should be regularly scheduled events. Someone in the department will have to plan the sessions and arrange for speakers. Keeping up-to-date on the collection, services and searching techniques is more difficult for librarians with part-time assignments in the reference department (working part-time or having part of their time assigned elsewhere) because they have less time to devote to the activity. They can request that training sessions be offered when they can attend or that they are funded for training. Also, they can make sure that their responsibilities leave them time for keeping current.

If reference librarians are concerned about the service they give the student, they will be alert to other ways in which they keep prepared for desk service. One way librarians can do this is by following up on questions they referred with the librarian receiving the referral. Another way is for the librarian to consult another librarian about how they might approach the same question more effectively. By exchanging ideas, both librarians in these situations will sharpen their approach to similar questions at a later time. Further suggestions about preparedness are discussed later.

*Chapter 10.*

# Reference Manuals

Reference manuals can make it easier for librarians to assist patrons at the desk. They can be in several parts; for example, one might be divided into sections on information, procedures, policy statements, and codes of ethics. They can include any information which supports the librarian on the desk.

Reference desk manuals are time consuming to prepare and require maintenance to keep them up to date. They probably should be contained in loose leaf notebooks. An outline system which allows for changes and expansion can be worked out so that parts can be revised individually without affecting other parts. The topics in each section should have their own numbered pages. A table of contents and index can be provided.

Procedures and policies can be distributed as memos, but they need to be collected and placed at the desk with an index to them. It may be that every reference librarian feels a need to keep a personal collection of all memos as well.[1]

## Information and Procedure Manuals

Information and procedure manuals provide quick-find information such as call numbers for foreign language dictionaries and table or shelf location of indexes and abstracts. Some information usually found in a manual can be mounted on the public access online catalog.[2]

The following library information and procedures should be included in a reference desk manual: How to fill out the forms used for book requests from storage or interlibrary loan and which desk to take them to. Lists of subject specialists or bibliographers. Lists of language specialists in the library for assistance or translation. Lists of professional typists for theses and dissertations. Emergency information (what to do in case of a bomb threat, for example). Indexes to periodical indexes and CD-ROMs by specific subject giving table or shelf location. Where to send away for full texts of patents. Who owns the microfiche of materials cited in the ASI indexes. Call numbers for language dictionaries. Some of this information could be listed in the public online catalog as well.

The manual can also contain information prepared for training sessions on important or rarely used tools, identified only through a bibliography.[3] Materials in the Sabin collection of books about America might be an example. Even now, it is impossible for the present author and other reference librarians to remember if the fiche containing the texts can be looked up directly in the file alphabetically or whether the bibliography either in print form or on microfiche must be used.[4] This information can be contained in a desk manual. As mentioned in the discussion on Internet, information about what is available and how to find the information could be placed in the manual.

A list of who does what in the library is useful. If a user needs an uncataloged book immediately, to whom do reference librarians make the request? What about catalog errors? Whom do they tell? Is there a procedure? What do librarians tell someone who wishes to recommend a book? Other possibilities: An organization chart. A list of faculty members on the library committee. Officers of the library friends. Information and procedures for nonaffiliated borrowers: Can they obtain cards and check out materials?[5] Committees or task forces in the department. The officers of the librarian association. Who is in charge of problems with which equipment or whom does the librarian call if the lavatory overflows? The manual should include the publications of the various units in the library to answer informational questions.

Much of this information could be memorized or learned, but new reference librarians will find it helpful to have at their fingertips in a well-indexed manual. In some cases memorizing it all is needless if the information can be quickly looked up in a procedure manual. Much of the information in the reference desk manual can be duplicated in an information desk manual.

As part of reference manuals, but possibly separate from them, are files which list difficult or often-asked questions. Questions can be recorded for the acquisitions librarian or for use by other members of the department. The record of the question should include the date entered, source of information and name of librarian contributing the information.[6] Some libraries maintain a record of these questions in a file or notebook. Recently the University of California at Los Angeles has made them available online.[7] The main criterion is that they be readily used.

Other libraries have developed indexes to assist the librarian at the desk, such as indexes to the periodical indexes in the reference collection or the reference collection itself[8] or indexes to local newspapers or special collection information.[9] These may be free-standing or part of the manual.

## Policy Statements

Policy statements are helpful in providing uniform standards of service of the highest quality to patrons and a basis for continuity in a department.[10] They can assist the librarian in decision-making by providing guidelines and written support, particularly when a difficult patron is asking for an out-of-the-ordinary service such as permission to check out one volume of a multivolume encyclopedia.

Academic library reference departments should have written policy statements to cover the services they offer and to which patrons. Reference departments are not alone in needing policy statements for service. Many service organizations outside the library profession (governmental agencies and retail stores, for example) have policies on such things as telephone callers. In a 1992 *Library Journal* article, Strickler discusses his experience with service policy in a bookstore.[11]

Even in reference departments that do not have written policy statements, reference librarians will undoubtedly operate on the basis of unwritten policies. Without written statements, there will be differences of opinion about policies among librarians who serve on a desk, and thus inconsistencies in service which could be harmful not only to the reference department, but to the library as a whole.

Librarians have enough difficulty applying policies when they are written down without the needless anxiety of either being unsure when to apply a policy or having to clarify policy often with the head of the department. Without written policies, the reference managers will be making ad hoc decisions on policy when questions are brought to them.

The reference policies could cover something as obvious as not giving answers off the top of the head to how far from the desk librarians should go in helping a student. Other examples might include the answers to such questions as the following:[12] What kind of telephone service do we offer? What kind of service do we provide to users not affiliated with the campus? Do we charge them for services? Do we consider the extracurricular needs of our basic clientele?[13]

Lynch, in an article on reference policy, discusses the activities needing policies which were considered by a committee at the University of Massachusetts and the answers she received from a request to ARL libraries for their policy statements. She appended a draft outline of a reference service policy manual.[14] More recently ACRL has prepared a document "Guidelines for the Preparation of Policies on Library Access," which includes a section on "Access to Services."[15] In 1982, Bill Katz published a compendium of policy statements from universities throughout the country.[16] It includes information about preparing statements.

Lynch's outline has an introduction, a section on type of services in general, library users, priorities, desk service policies and instruction, interlibrary loan, bibliographical services, reference correspondence, documentation, orientation and instruction. At the present time, policy statements include online searching, use of Internet and CD-ROMs. Especially important to discuss are what Lynch says about nature and extent of responsibilities for desk duty and her guidelines for behavior and attitudes.

# NATURE AND EXTENT OF RESPONSIBILITIES

Policy statements should define the level of service which reference librarians will offer. The level of service may be different for various clienteles of a library: faculty, undergraduate students, graduate students, staff and outsiders. If the president or chancellor of the institution or head of the library needs information, even the head of reference may drop everything and search anywhere in the library for the information or even call another library. Blind or almost blind and otherwise handicapped patrons or faculty members with aching backs may receive added service such as finding books on the shelves for them.

# BEHAVIOR AND ATTITUDES

In their policy statements or in a separate statement, some reference departments have written standards for performance at the desk explaining the behavior and attitudes expected of reference librarians. Besides listing the standard, the physical actions which demonstrate the guidelines are usually spelled out.[17]

Here are a couple of examples:

> Standard: Reference Desk staff convey an attitude and manner that encourages users to seek assistance.
> Indicators: Acknowledgment of people who approach the desk or are waiting for service (when staff are occupied with another user). People who seem to need help are offered assistance.

> Standard: Assistance is provided at the appropriate level of need.
> Indicator: Ability to determine the real question; continued questioning to be sure the problem is understood. Alternative sources are suggested, including other libraries or non-library sources.[18]

Larson and Dickson have reported on "Developing Behavioral Reference Performance Standards" at the University of Nebraska.[19] Their study could be used as a model in the development of standards. They identified five goals for reference service and then found it relatively easy to group desired behaviors under them.

Standards can be used by librarians for measurement of their own performance because they present an objective view of desk performance, for a program of peer evaluation to improve departmental performance, or for use by heads of departments when they must make an evaluation for the purpose of merit increases, promotion or retention.[20] For the heads of reference departments, standards make an excellent basis for discussions of performance and needs for improvement. They can provide a basis for training a new librarian. The development of standards by a department can promote teamwork and enhance morale.

Since the profession as a whole felt that it was advantageous to have standards for public service so that reference services could be examined quantitatively and qualitatively, a document establishing guidelines for service was prepared in 1976 by the Reference and Adult Services Division of the American Library Association and revised in 1979.[21] Klassen remarked in his comments on these early guidelines, "They gave little by the way of quantitative or qualitative measures by which libraries might evaluate their services … the guidelines emphasized areas of reference service that were well established in practice."[22] The guidelines evoked some other criticism and comments, but were still useful for librarians to consider in planning their service programs.[23] In 1990, new guidelines were published, constituting "a statement of service goals rather than a codification of practices."[24] They were written with an expanded view of information services and could be used along with the earlier statements in analyzing a reference or library service program.

These guidelines addressed primarily the types of service that should be offered to users. Most recently, an ad hoc Committee on Behavioral Guidelines for Reference and Information Services was appointed by the then president of the Reference and Adult Services Division of the American Library Association.[25] The charge to the committee was to develop a set of behavioral guidelines. "These guidelines will recommend the behaviors an individual librarian should exhibit when responding to an individual patron's information needs."[26] The committee's report was accepted by the RASD directors at the ALA midwinter meeting 1996. The Guidelines will be published in *RQ* Winter issue 1997. As representative of the profession's collective wisdom, these guidelines should take advantage of the work that has been done at various reference departments throughout the country.

## Code of Ethics

A code of ethics might be even more difficult to draft than statements of policies and standards, when one considers that "Ethical problems are ones that do not have easy answers."[27] Professional ethics have long been discussed in the literature and continue to be discussed.[28]

It has been said that "One hallmark of a profession is a code of ethics."[29] As a professional organization, the American Library Association has had a code of ethics for many years. The latest edition for 1981 was developed in order that fair, equitable and unbiased service be given.[30] While it contains useful guidelines, the code of ethics is perhaps not specific enough for librarians to follow in their day-to-day work.

In fact, Gremmels challenges the code's guidelines, saying they are based on a rights theory rather than a communitarian theory.[31] In the latter theory the common good is upheld over individual rights. Under the rights theory, a librarian should not refuse to help a patron looking for information on how to make a bomb or how to make freebase cocaine, but following communitarian theory the librarian could refuse to assist on the grounds that the information would be harmful to the public good.

There are other issues which the code of ethics does not address in the areas of helping patrons, purchasing materials, confidentiality and privacy. Should one help paid assistants or parents doing someone else's work? Is it proper to borrow a controversial book you would not buy? How much help should one give a commercial information broker? What about fair use of reference service for assignments, or more specifically for library school students?[32]

The code of ethics also does not address personal ethical problems such as service when sick, disproportionate personal taking credit for joint efforts (or accepting it when it is not due), reading best sellers before patrons, free copying privileges, and relaxation of overdue fines for librarians. What about accepting gifts, including entertainment?

Questions about confidentiality and the right to privacy might include the following: What about the confidentiality of circulation records when someone else needs the book? What about helping someone who you know is duplicating someone else's research? What about the use of patron questions for library instruction or training sessions? What about keeping lists of difficult questions or a record of online subject searches?

In her article in the section on current issues on Reference and Adult Services, Futas asks for feedback in order to open up discussion of situations which require ethical judgments.[33] It is to be assumed that there will be more discussion in the literature on ethics in general and in special areas of librarianship which could also be generally useful.[34]

Reference librarians are required to make many subjective judgments, including ethical ones. A reference manual which includes some discussion of professional ethics can assist reference librarians in their decisions.

# PART III.

# Other Reference Activities

Since many libraries are reorganizing reference services by tiering their service, with library assistants answering the first layer of questions, and some are eliminating reference desk service entirely, services which reference librarians perform while not on duty at a desk are now even more important than ever.[1] It is apparent even without the present trend toward desk elimination or division that off-desk activities have increased in extent and complexity in the past twenty or more years and will continue to be a major part of the activities of reference librarians in the future.[2] These activities present the reference librarian with a fragmented workload and a need for more diverse skills and knowledge.

Reference librarians have rarely spent every minute of every day assigned to a desk except perhaps on weekends when they may be assigned for an eight-hour stint. In fact, most full-time librarians spend no more than 30 to 50 percent of their time assigned to a desk even when the weekend hours are factored in[3] or when the hours which they spend substituting for their colleagues are considered.[4] Public librarians and academic librarians on smaller campuses spend more hours on the desk than their colleagues on larger campuses, but they still are not usually assigned to desk duty the full 35–40 hours that they work.[5]

The duties which reference librarians perform off the desk depend to a large extent on their library's goals and objectives for service to its patrons and for its total program. The distribution of the activities depends on the library's priorities and what it expects of its librarians in terms of library, university and professional service or of research and scholarship.

Librarians' obligations off the desk are usually not assigned tasks to be carried out as requested. More likely, as professionals, librarians will be charged with responsibility for parts of the services program with a great deal of leeway as to when and how they carry out their assignments. In this way, they will be determining the library policy within guidelines on how their time—i.e., their salary—is spent. Very few librarians will be told precisely what to do.

While librarians are assigned to a service station a rather constant number of hours during the week, how they spend their hours off the desk may vary widely from week to week. Librarians adjust their own time and set their own priorities among their responsibilities. For example, if they make several presentations to classes in any one week, they may accomplish very little collection development that week, or obviously when librarians attend an ALA conference, for example, their normal duties including their desk hours will have to be covered by another librarian.

Assignments in a reference department are usually tailored to the qualifications of individual librarians. When the staff changes, the assignments in the department will change, for a new member may not have the same abilities as the person departing. Yearly reviews may indicate a need for realignments of duties because someone may no longer be effective. Assignments might be orientation, instruction, publications, reference collection, electronic collection and equipment, desk supervision, and so on. The head of reference or of public services should review assignments to make sure all are covered, taking into account new opportunities for service.

Most libraries have extensive programs already in place, but it is important to examine the effectiveness of those programs to determine whether they are successful and whether changes would be useful in improving service. This examination of services may take the form of a full-scale analysis worked out with professional consultants, such as the Office of Management Services of the Association of Research Libraries. These consultants can present a framework for library staffs to understand how what is being done in services compares to what could be done. A review of this nature can be useful in the evaluation and planning process for a library.

Some issues may require library-wide debate with input from the reference staff. It is most effective for a library to have a master plan for service against which to consider recommendations or through which effective programs and priorities can be assigned.

As part of their analysis of academic programs and resultant user needs, reference librarians, in particular, will collectively work out programs to satisfy the needs identified: classes, workshops, publications.

Several specific instances of response to individual academic programs will indicate what can be done in adapting to identified academic programs:

• A recurring assignment in several history classes requires students to read a book and find a review of it and biographical information on the author before writing their own critique. To assist students with the assignment, a reference department might prepare a leaflet to explain how to locate book reviews and also one to assist the students in finding biographical information. A department might also prepare a slide/tape show or video to demonstrate how students might find their reviews and biographies. The faculty members making the assignment could be contacted by a librarian to determine whether they might like a presentation at the time the assignment is initiated.

• When a library discovers that the Department of Speech and Hearing requires their majors to take Library Skills (1 unit) and Library Research (2 units), librarians could develop a course to meet more specifically the research needs of students in the speech and hearing program, an interdisciplinary field that makes use of indexes in the field of medicine, psychology and education among others.

• When the arts library for space reasons must put material in storage, rather than select material throughout the library to go to storage, it decides to store the major portion of the books in the NK classification (Decorative Arts) as a response to the program in the art department because no specific classes are taught in this field.

• When the instructor of an introductory psychology class

decides that the students need help in library research, the library works with the instructor and teaching assistants in presenting a session on finding materials in the library, showing a slide tape show on *Psychological Abstracts* and its related electronic databases and preparing a search strategy handout for the students. Handouts or bibliographies are often prepared for class presentations by librarians tailored to classes such as how a law is enacted or sources for the study of German literature.

• A CD-ROM with access to information in Chicano studies is purchased to serve a strong Chicano department because it is recognized that this specific index will provide a single place to look for information on Chicano people and culture rather than using many other indexes which might or might not contain the desired information.

*Chapter 11.*

# Collection Responsibilities

*Reference Collection*

A major activity of reference librarians when not on desk duty is the management and development of the reference collection. Among the responsibilities of a reference department, the collection ranks second only to direct personal service. Without resources for an inquiry, reference librarians will not be able to perform competently. The collection must be managed and developed. Management involves the determination of the size, location, and arrangement of the collection, as well as the maintenance of its materials; while development entails selection and deselection of materials and filling the needs for special collections. The development and management of the collection may be in the hands of one librarian or may be assigned to several.

The size of the reference collection may be predetermined by the floor space assigned to it. On the other hand, the optimum size for the collection sometimes determines the space requirements in the building. Small colleges and universities will tend to have small reference collections, whereas large libraries have large collections. The number of volumes may range from a few thousand volumes to 25,000 or 30,000 volumes or more.[1] Once the size of the collection has been fixed, evaluation of materials for weeding needs to take place at regular intervals.[2] The size of reference desk collections may be worked out in a similar way.

The collection and electronic reference sources need to be reasonably close to the reference desk and be arranged in such a way that librarians at the desk can observe the various areas in order to identify and assist students needing help. They need to be close enough so that librarians do not become exhausted walking to them or opt not to take the time to accompany students to the sources.

## *Arrangement of Collection*

The reference collection itself can be completely arranged by call number or be divided into separate sections for indexes and abstracts, encyclopedias, biography, bibliography, etc. Within the confines of the area allotted, the material should be arranged for easy access and convenience of use. Heavily used materials can be placed on tables, or the shelves can be low so that their surface can be used for examining materials, or table-like shelves can be provided in the stack area. The location of individual resources and their arrangement must be constantly reviewed to make sure that they are working for the department and the students.

However the materials are arranged in the reference area, the users must be made aware of the arrangement through signs, posters or lists. Even though, for example, indexes and abstracts are placed on tables or shelves in call number order, users, and librarians as well, may need help finding them.[3] Some students will have had a skills class or a library session in another class or will be clever about using self-help leaflets, posters, and signs. Others will wander aimlessly, vaguely looking for what they want. It is these students that the librarians at the desk will have to watch for. Some students, of course, will come to the desk and ask when they need help.

In addition to the main reference collection, most libraries will have small desk collections for ready reference. Constant use of some sources by librarians at the desk will be the usual reason for establishing a ready reference collection, but some librarians place materials on ready reference to keep the materials from disappearing. Small college libraries are less likely to have ready reference desk collections, but nearly all large university reference departments will have them. The size of the collections may vary from 30 to 250 volumes. In a library with a large reference collection dispersed over a large area, the ready reference collection will tend to grow if only from the weariness of librarians having to walk long distances for some materials.[4]

Ready reference material will include sources for answering frequently asked factual questions, special tools for librarians, up-to-date directories and the like. Sometimes heavily used reference materials are placed in the ready reference collection to prevent theft, loss or damage. Standard texts such as the Bible may also be included in the collection.

## Development of the Collections

In some libraries, catalogers or subject specialists decide what shall be placed in general reference. However, if the reference department is to have a collection which can provide for the needs of the students in pursuing their course work or research and simultaneously aid reference librarians in giving assistance, someone in the reference department must be responsible for coordinating the acquisition of reference materials and their management. While ultimately the head of the department may be responsible, collection development and management may be delegated to someone else in the department. This assignment will be one of coordination since many reference librarians and subject specialists will be identifying the needs of the students for reference materials and making recommendations. Besides coordinating requests from others, the coordinator will have to insure that subject, interdisciplinary and general reference works are acquired to support the reference program.

## Reference Collection Policy Statements

Reference librarians prepare, as subject specialists have done for the rest of the collection, policy statements for what is collected for reference purposes based on the educational program as well as on the knowledge of tools actually consulted to assist the student.[5] Subject specialists determine the level of collecting, from minimal to comprehensive, to be accomplished in various subjects. In developing the policy for a reference collection, it must be recognized that the reference collections may need to go beyond the collection levels for the academic programs in providing access to materials that are not owned by the library. In order to provide access, libraries purchase heavily in the field of bibliography.

The reference collection policy should state the categories in which the library is to collect, and should specify language, format, and number of copies required. Frequency of purchase of new editions must be addressed in the policy: every year, every three years or longer. Amount of revision, timeliness of data for the student, value in the collection and funding enter into these decisions. For example, because most libraries cannot afford to buy new encyclopedias every year, they purchase them on a rotating basis so that not all of the encyclopedias are purchased in the same year. The collection of electronic databases and their software also needs to be addressed in the guidelines: Will the databases be purchased and mounted on the public access catalog? Will a CD-ROM network be installed, or will single stations be set up for their use?

The policy should address the question of weeding, giving criteria for discarding or moving material to the regular stacks or storage.[6] To some extent weeding is automatic: when a new edition arrives, the older edition goes to the stacks unless it is not completely replaced by the new edition. Weeding of a collection usually has low priority, but since it is important to have a usable and up-to-date collection, the librarian in charge of selection needs to weed outdated materials. Criteria for weeding include frequency of use, age of material, and the arrival of new editions. Publishers may also ask that old materials be returned or destroyed. The decision to discard materials may be based on the need for them in the future for research or their use for instructional purposes.[7]

The reference collection policy should include statements about which special collections will be owned or supervised. These might include the microform collections, government documents, newspapers, vertical file materials such as pamphlets or annual reports, telephone directories, and college catalogs. Maintenance of these collections is time consuming for librarians and library assistants.

If collected, pamphlets will have to be selected and deselected because they are generally of use only if they contain current information. They will have to be filed and refiled after they have circulated. Keeping college catalogs and telephone directories in order and available is an endless task. Some libraries have replaced college catalogs with microfiche collections even though they are awkward for the user. Many have replaced telephone directories with CD-ROMs or have decided not to offer the service.

A reference collection policy should determine the criteria for placing something on ready reference, rather than by arbitrary accumulations of materials. Biggs sets forth criteria for placing works in a ready reference collection.[8] At Mankato State University, achieving a consensus on criteria for what should be on ready reference proved a good opportunity for the library's reference department to work collegially.[9]

## Selection of Materials

Reference materials may be purchased on standing order for serials and new editions, through approval plans or through individual selection. In libraries with approval plans, the reference collection coordinator and subject specialists for their areas review materials received or citations for materials as they come into the library. The coordinator and subject specialists make sure that the approval plan has not missed important materials.

Even with an approval plan, the coordinator will review the advertisements, scan major journals for possible titles and compare acquisitions for the library with the lists of best reference works for the year as they are published. Where approval plans are not used, reference librarians may use these methods for selection.

In fact, in some cases, reference librarians may wish to read reviews before adding a work which has come in on approval or which they are considering ordering, even though reviews are often delayed and selection must be made without their guidance. Selection will follow the reference collection policy for the library. Subject area of the reference work in relation to the subject program at the school, the quality of the publisher, ease of use, indexes provided, duplication with other works, and accuracy are further criteria for selection of reference works.[10]

The librarian in charge of selecting materials may be assigned a budget for the purchase of reference materials. The coordinator will have to keep within the budget. In a time of tightening budgets this may mean deselection particularly of serials. Negotiating with subject specialists about purchases may be a major responsibility for this librarian. In library systems with branches, the collection developer in the reference department will have to work with the collection development librarian for the branches to decide which works will be duplicated. Faced with purchasing multiple sets of, say, *Chemistry Abstracts* or *Psychological Abstracts* in paper or CD-ROM format, they must make decisions even if the decision ends up being to eliminate a branch. The position of coordinator of the reference collection requires highly developed professional judgment.

## *Maintenance*

While much of the work of maintenance can be turned over to library assistants or students, the librarian in charge of the collection will have to make sure that the work is carried out: proper labeling and recording of location, inventory, bindery scheduling, and possibly the maintenance of a reference shelf list or an online record that contains the information needed to identify a given work as reference material and indicate its placement in a special location. Most reference periodicals will have to be bound at slow times of the year and on a rush basis according to a procedure set up by the coordinator and the binding unit in the library.

While most libraries have abandoned inventorying their whole collection, the reference collection needs periodic inventory checks to make sure that the materials needed are on the shelves. Missing items are usually identified when the first reference librarian who wishes to use one of them cannot locate it on the shelf. However, with the tendency of reference books on open shelves, particularly heavily used ones, to move around the library, it may be difficult for the librarian to know whether a book is just off the shelf or missing. The inventory and searching can be assigned to students or library assistants, but the coordinator in consultation with other reference librarians will have to decide whether to replace missing items.

Some reference departments annotate the bibliographies of collected works with the library's call number. It is useful for students when they use a collected work such as Granger's *Index to Poetry* or the *Short Story Index* to have the call number written in the work so that each person using the bibliography does not have to check the catalogs for the call numbers. For librarians using Sheehy's *Guide to Reference Books*, it may be useful to have the call number of the works owned by the library written in.

While usually accomplished by student assistants during the summer months, annotations are another time consuming activity which requires updating as new editions arrive. Maintenance of annotations in collected works may be becoming a relic of the past when there were fewer demands on librarians' and assistants' time.

Some libraries index their local newspapers or clip newspapers for local history files. Some may index the collection of indexes and abstracts or CD-ROMs by subject. Each library must decide what aids are helpful for the use of their collections and, more important, whether it has the staff and funds to produce the aids. Indexes may be printed or computer produced or be online.

## Subject Collections

Libraries must have collections that serve the needs of their academic community. During the sixties, many libraries were building idealized research collections to serve current and future needs, but when the crunch came at the end of the decade, they turned their attention more squarely to collecting for the immediate research needs of their campuses and to the task of providing equally for the academic requirements of their undergraduate constituency.[11]

To match their collections to the needs of the academic

communities, libraries appointed collection development librarians who studied the academic programs and discussed needs with the faculty and then developed collection policy statements for the subject areas for which they were responsible. Collection development librarians determined at which level materials in their individual subject fields would be collected—whether exhaustive, research, reference or skeletal—and in what format (print, microform, online or CD-ROM.[12]

As another solution, libraries entered consortia and developed cooperative collecting and lending agreements to obtain materials for the more esoteric needs of their students through interlibrary loan. Cooperative purchasing on a nationwide basis had been going on for many years prior to the introduction of online facilities.

Individual libraries agreed to have exhaustive collections in certain areas—for example, the total output from a smaller country. In providing for this cooperation at the present time, libraries which are members of the Research Libraries Group have prepared collection evaluations using the RLG conspectus indicating what materials they own and collect in specific subject areas. Access to the conspectus information is available through the RLIN (Research Libraries Information Network) database.

Academic libraries have assigned the selection responsibilities for the collection to subject specialists, who are sometimes organized into groups for coordination of purchasing in interdisciplinary areas and for dissemination of information and training. Some very large libraries have subject bibliographers for collection development, but most libraries assign collection development as one of the duties of catalogers or reference librarians. Thus most reference librarians have subject collection responsibilities. They not only select materials in a subject area, but act as a resource person on that subject for the rest of the library.

The collection part of their job follows the policies and procedures for collection development of the library. It includes selection as well as weeding, including cancellation of subscriptions and determining what should go into storage.

As with the selection of reference materials, reference librarians review the books and citations from approval plans for their subject field as well as the literature which discusses new materials. In performing these duties, librarians must maintain close contact with the faculty in their subject departments on campus. They will have to know what is taught in the undergraduate and graduate areas as well as the specialties of the faculty. With this information the librarian will not only be able to determine which books to add to the collection, but which faculty members to approach with instructional proposals and how to assist them with current awareness of new library materials and service. When it comes to canceling subscriptions and putting materials in storage, it would be foolhardy for subject collectors not to receive the widest possible input from the faculty.

It is ironic that with less money to spend, more time has to be spent on selection. Depending on the size of the department, the emphasis the school places on the subject department, the expertise of the librarian, and library constraints such as budget and use of jobbers, subject specialists may spend as little as 5 percent to as much as 20 percent or more of their time on collection development.

As subject specialists, reference librarians may report to managers of collection development rather than to the head of reference for this part of their activities. Some libraries recognize that reference librarians may have two separate job assignments by having one librarian in charge of both services and collection development. Actually, since subject specialists function as both collection developers and service persons for the area of their expertise, it may be difficult to separate those portions of a librarian's job because they intermesh.

*Chapter 12.*

# Instruction

The discussion here and in the next chapter documents the types of programs reference librarians have set up to provide instruction in the use of the library. These basic types of programs likely will continue to be used in the future, though their substance is sure to change over time and they may eventually be renamed, perhaps as information literacy education.

The major programs which reference librarians provide off the desk are instructional. Whether the academic library should offer instruction to their patrons has been argued back and forth in the literature of librarianship for a considerable length of time.[1] In the mid-nineties, the value of bibliographic instruction is once again being debated.[2]

The debate about librarians as teachers has spread out into the arguments for and against faculty status. At least one librarian feels that faculty status is beside the point. Swan states in a letter to the editor of the *Library Journal*, "librarians must think like teachers, not out of envy or 'status seeking,' but in order to be good librarians."[3]

Early arguments for librarians taking part in teaching programs were the value of education in which individual learning is emphasized and the view that instruction in the use of libraries is a cost effective method of providing assistance to huge student bodies. From libraries' point of view, instructional programs make it possible to teach students in a group setting rather than individually. By relabeling bibliographic instruction as information literacy in the new technological environment, it would seem even more important for librarians to offer instruction to students.

Until recently most service librarians in a university setting had only one answer to the "instruction or not" question. They were convinced they had to teach the students to become self-sufficient library users so that the students would be successful in pursuing knowledge during their college career and in their life after graduation. In an academic institution, it seemed imperative not just to assist students, but to teach them about how the informational literature of a subject is produced and structured and because of its structure, how it is accessed.

In our complex modern world, students need to know how to use libraries as early as possible in their college career so that they will be able to find information effectively while they are students and after they graduate. This emphasis on instruction seems to be the current philosophy of service in the academic library in spite of the questions being raised.[4] Now, instead of use of the library, the term "access to information" is appropriate since information may be accessed either in the library or from a remote location. Programs that target remote users may be difficult to design.

While there may be a whole raft of reasons for instruction being offered at a given school, the main reason that instruction in the use of libraries developed was to satisfy an observed need of students. When the needs change, librarians redesigned programs to meet the new needs. Librarians saw that students were perplexed and daunted by the information riches in the academic library. Reference librarians were inundated by repetitive questions at the desk which could be answered in group presentations or in leaflets rather than individually.

They could see that if the basic mechanics of library use were taught, students might be able to move on to further use of library resources for research. They recognized that if they taught students about the methodology for library research, students would find library research easier and would produce better research results. They were appalled when graduate students turned in their dissertations and were stunned to discover that they had not known of sources and means of access to sources which would have made their work easier and saved them vast amounts of time.

Once instructional programs were under way, librarians discovered that some faculty members were unaware of methods of access and sources which could assist them with their class preparations and research. Librarians not only identified the need for education in the use of the library, but recognized it was their responsibility rather than that of faculty members to teach students the use of the library. They had to figure out how to instruct their patrons.

Librarians determined that for the bewildered freshman student, instruction needed to be both affective and cognitive. In order to use the library successfully, new students needed to feel confident in their ability to use major access tools in the library and to locate materials in the library. This confidence meant that students would be at ease in looking for information as well as feeling comfortable about asking a librarian for assistance.

Although it would appear that with the development of electronic information sources, there would be less need for instruction, in actuality more teaching may be required to inform students about online catalogs, CD-ROMs and online databases and guide them in the use of new databases and equipment.[5] Using electronic information sources which are not completely conducive to self-help, both students and faculty have become more receptive to library instruction. Students need to know not just how to handle the electronic environment, but when to use which systems, how to translate their needs to the system and how to evaluate the results. No matter how user friendly a system is, students will still have to be taught problem solving for satisfying their academic needs.

Joanne Euster seems to have the best answer to the question, Does bibliographic instruction have a legitimate place in the academic library? She says, "The question is rather: in which way should students be taught to use the library and to locate and use information?"[6]

University libraries, and smaller college libraries as well, use a multiplicity of ways of educating their patrons, for even at a small institution the student body is diverse enough to require many different approaches.[7] Students have a wide variety of interests as well as different levels of ability in using the library as an adjunct to their course work. As students progress through their four or more years at a school, they will have different skill levels and different needs. Also in any student body, students will have a wide range of learning styles.[8] Some students learn best by reading, some by listening and others by doing.

## *Planning*

To address student diversity in all its manifestations, a library needs an instructional plan. The plan may provide for classes, in-class presentations, informal tours and workshops and publications.

While it is possible for instruction programs to develop like Topsy (just grow), it makes sense to ascertain the needs of the patrons and develop a plan to meet these needs. A plan was recommended in the "Guidelines for Information Services" of 1979.[9] As Cottam states it, "From planning come better design and more responsive programs. Planning clarifies needs, goals, objectives, procedures, and methods, and it paves the way for evaluation and improvement."[10] An example of an extensive plan is the one developed by the University of Texas at Austin.[11] The plan identifies all users and the instruction needed for them at various levels. Before the librarians developed their plan, they surveyed both the faculty, to determine their attitudes toward library instruction and services to students, and the students themselves, to determine needs and interests. They also surveyed librarians about their attitudes and instructional programs. Goals were then developed for specific user groups in terms of awareness, orientation and bibliographic instruction. A detailed plan was worked out to meet the needs of all three areas. A plan can be developed following the guidelines worked out by the Association of College and Research Libraries.[12]

The 1987 model statement was shaped around the following eight categories: user groups targeted by objectives, ordering of objectives, institution and tool specific information, language used, incorporation of technological advances, evaluation of information sources and systems, evaluation of objectives, and structural flexibility. Its detail made the statement more useful than the earlier guidelines.[13]

An instructional plan should target user groups, students, graduate students, faculty, foreign students, etc., and supply what each group needs in terms of user awareness, orientation, and knowledge of how to use and do research in a library. In the process of developing a plan in addition to actual teaching, publications will be identified that are needed to support the instructional program.

## Coordination

While it is possible for the head of the reference department to develop a plan and direct a program of bibliographic instruction, it is more effective, whenever possible, to assign the coordination of library instruction to one person either within the reference department or directly under the administrator for public service.[14] Since so much can be included (as is being done in this book) under the umbrella of library instruction, conceivably the coordination or the responsibility for parts of the program could be split up and assigned to several librarians supervised by the head of the reference department or other unit heads.

To some extent the responsibility for instruction is shared with the faculty. Thus, parts of the instructional program are best developed in consultation with the faculty or with the faculty's advice and support. Library instruction is more effective with faculty support. Librarians may need to have faculty help in receiving approval of proposed credit courses, particularly if a course must find a home in an academic department.

Librarians will need to work with the faculty on presentations about using the library for individual classes, both in arranging a time for the presentation and in the development of the content and assignments. However, unless librarians mount their own courses in bibliographic access, they are only able to give instruction on the basis of the goodwill of faculty members.

The advantages of a coordinator are in the realm of planning and preparation. The responsibilities of the coordinator may include all the activities discussed in this section; for example, developing credit courses, teaching or working with those who teach, preparing textbooks, planning training sessions of all sorts, promoting and supporting in-class instruction, acting as a clearinghouse for orientation and instruction tours, and preparing and assisting with the preparation of materials for instructional sessions. Coordinators will need the support of their colleagues, both informally and through advisory committees. They will also need clerical assistance.[15]

For an instructional program it is useful to have an instructional center where materials can be collected and shared. While the instructional coordinator's office can serve as the instructional center, the office does not serve the purpose very well. Librarians are not as apt to file their materials in the center because they see it as the coordinator's office and not as a facility that they share. Not only is a place for materials needed, but also a place to store equipment for the programs, preferably under lock and key.

## *Classroom*

A classroom area of some sort within the library for instructional presentations to both large and small groups is usually essential for an instructional program. Students need to associate bibliographic instruction with the library. Also, it can be cumbersome for librarians to take reference sources they need for their presentations elsewhere on the campus. While secluded areas of the library can be used for small groups, presentations tend to disturb users in the area. However, a library needs to be careful about labeling rooms that are used for these purposes as classrooms lest the campus administration latch onto the room and schedule classes in it. Ideally the classroom should be equipped with workstations so that students can have hands-on practice in searching the online catalog or other databases. At a minimum there needs to be a computer, a telephone line and modem, and a liquid crystal display unit for demonstration purposes.

## Planning Instructional Programs

Some types of programs that can be developed will be now be discussed. However, this examination is not intended to be a "how to" manual, but rather an overview of ways to meet the multiplicity of demands. There is a great deal of information in the library literature on all aspects of instruction from planning to implementation and evaluations.[16] Librarians can make use of colleagues' programs in planning and designing their own instructional programs.

Bibliographic instruction librarians promote using available materials by saying "there is no reason to reinvent the wheel." Besides the literature, there are clearinghouses throughout the country with instructional materials[17] as well as the national LOEX (Library Orientation Exchange) and ERIC (Educational Resources Information Center) files.[18] The latter's materials can be found using ERIC's printed indexes, online databases or CD-ROMs.[19] A newsletter LOEX publishes allows solicitation of specific kinds of material and informs librarians about new materials that are available in the file. Librarians can also write to LOEX for specific types of material or topics. At the present time through BITNET, an electronic network, assistance or information can be requested and supplied by electronic mail.[20] Also, most bibliographic instruction librarians are happy to share their experience and methodologies, either by sending material or by giving workshops.

## Orientation

Although orientation can be considered the first level of instruction, the library has an obligation prior to orientation; that is, to inform the student body of library services, to make the students aware of the library as a source of information. Before students can use a library at all, they need to recognize the library as a source of information and know something about its facilities and services.

To meet this need, information about the library can be presented in campus orientation tours, in the freshman and transfer student introductory packets, in the student newspaper orientation issue or by academic counselors. Video or slide tape programs can be brought to dormitories. Advertisements of tours and classes can be published in the student newspaper.

Mostly, students are made aware of the library and its services through orientation programs. Libraries have always planned and made available orientation at all levels for their clientele. They have given tours, published guides and walking tours, and prepared slide tape shows, video presentations and audio tours.

Since the library is part of the overall campus of a university, the orientation of new students should be worked out in conjunction with those in charge of campus orientation. This might be arranged by library representation on planning groups. This coordination with other groups cannot be a once and forever thing because the campus itself changes its programs, renaming them or offering them at different times.

Most often orientation is offered at the beginning of the fall term or during the summer months. In some cases, the campus group includes this initial library orientation in its general programs. At other times, the orientation is offered by the library and scheduled during the general orientation activities. Sometimes library orientation is offered as part of specialized orientation programs.[21]

For the scheduled sessions offered by libraries, slide tape shows or video presentations can be combined with walk-through tours.[22] Published library guides, printed walking tours and how-to leaflets can be given out to those taking the tours.

During the first weeks of school, libraries can offer tours as well as introductory presentations on the online catalog, if there is one, independently of orientation programs. Such sessions on the online catalog come closer to instructional workshops, described later. Special groups can be targeted for orientation: foreign students, teaching assistants, campus tour leaders.

In some small colleges, diagnostic tests have been administered as part of the orientation program to identify those students who will need further training in the use of libraries. This test and the instructional follow-up are predicated on the idea that the students need at least minimal skills in using the library to have successful college careers. Small schools, either because of the smaller number of students or because they feel a more direct responsibility for their students, are perhaps more committed to instructing their students in the use of libraries. This is not to imply that large schools do not have the commitment, since many do, but they face squarely the problem of numbers.[23]

Printed and audio tours can be available for individual students when they decide they want a tour. Both of these will require a reasonable amount of time and funds to produce, but once a printed walking tour has been developed, little effort is needed to keep it up to date.

An audio tour necessitates the availability of listening equipment. The library will have to decide before the audio tour is developed whether students are motivated enough to walk around the library carrying a tape recorder and wearing earphones. The equipment for the audio tours will have to be maintained. Revision and updating is a bit more difficult for audio tours, particularly if the tape must be recorded outside the library. A printed tour is perhaps simpler.

Tours are usually provided on demand for groups ranging from graduate seminars to local elementary school classes and are usually tailor made for the requesting group. To provide this service, procedures making use of forms to record the request for the tours can be used. The tours can be assigned to a specific librarian who will then contact the person requesting the tour (listed on the form) to make arrangements. Thus, the librarian who is giving the tour can find out exactly what is expected from the tour. In making this contact, the librarian may discover that a full fledged instructional session would be more useful. There is but a fine line of distinction between the in-depth tour and an instructional session.

While any reference librarian should be able to lead a group through the library indicating service points and access to the collection, more preparation is needed for an in-depth session.

For faculty orientation, the library may want to publish a faculty library handbook informing the faculty about collections and services, explaining loan procedures and interlibrary loan procedures, how to recommend a book for purchase, whom to contact in the library for these recommendations, and how to request instructional sessions.

## *Types of Instruction*

There are multiple ways in which libraries can formally instruct their patrons: credit classes of various kinds, in-class presentations, and special workshop sessions.

The method chosen will in part be based on the goals and attitudes of the library and the politics within the library and the faculty. Most librarians within an academic setting will use a variety of means to instruct students.

If the goal of a library is to introduce essential library skills and particularly the use of an online catalog to a student body of 10,000 to 20,000 or so, at every level, methods will have to be adopted for reaching these numbers of students. If the goal is to prepare students for research in a subject area, a different approach will need to be taken.

### COURSES

If administrators believe that it is the library's responsibility to teach all students the skills necessary to use the library, they will probably wish to offer a course in research skills. The question of whether the course should be offered for credit must be addressed, as must the issue of whether this credit will stand alone or as part of the coursework for another class. If it is to be a credit course, it will have to be determined whether it will be an elective or a required class. Since noncredit classes offer students no incentive but to learn, they are best conceived as short-term classes with few sessions. Even with credit classes attendance can be a problem, particularly in those offered with few units or on a pass/no pass basis. Rewards or gimmicks can be used to encourage attendance, as for example by making it possible to obtain assignments only in person or by offering some special privileges to those who attend faithfully.

There are almost as many solutions for offering classes as there are institutions. Thus, the first task in instituting an instructional program is to study the politics within the library and on the campus. For any program, it is necessary to gain the support of the top administrators in the library. Likewise, the librarians who will be teaching in the program will have to be in favor of the program and, if at all possible, actively involved with the design of the program. At minimum, they should be able to give their input on it.

It is particularly important to have faculty members supporting instructional programs, both as individuals and as members of committees. Contact with the faculty can be developed on an individual basis, by library representation on faculty library committees or by subject specialists attending departmental meetings.

If a credit course is to be set up, the library must understand the steps necessary to have a course approved, and must determine whether the request will have to be sponsored by a faculty member. If this is the case the library will have to persuade a faculty member to carry the course proposal through the authorizing committees. If the school has a library school, the course can be set up within the school, which, of course, means working with the faculty of the library school.

There can be many configurations in the presentation of classes: a complete course or part of a course for freshman, or both as upper division instruction. If a complete class is not feasible, the library can approach the coordinators of a freshman level class which would be a good home for library instruction. By offering a course itself, the library maintains control of the class and takes full responsibility for educating the library user rather than being reliant upon the good wishes of a faculty member or department.

If the library is to offer a course, it will have to determine where the course will fit into the overall schedule of classes at the academic institution. Are there interdisciplinary classes offered at the school? Can the course be offered in the humanities program or the science program?

In some colleges, all academic courses are four units, making it difficult to institute a credit class for library instruction. In those schools, library skills and research strategies will have to be incorporated into another academic class. Some departments offering freshman classes will have no interest in giving any time to library skills or research, while others might be willing to use one or two class periods.

Various instructional programs have been designed to reach a large number of students with the least expenditure of funds (i.e., librarians' time). The self-paced workbook has been one means universities have used for instruction. Workbooks and assignments are developed, along with enrollment procedures, grading and evaluations. Answer sheets that can be quickly graded either visually or electronically (the latter via Scantron sheets) have been used.

Because the student does the work on his own, it is necessary to address the problem of students actually doing their own work (not cheating). Various solutions have been worked out—for example, multiple question variations[24] and the use of several alternate questions for the lesson, changing every quarter.[25] Variations make it more difficult to use time-saving methods of grading.

While a workbook program will require quite a bit of one librarian's time, the load on other librarians should be minimal. However, because the students know they can receive help at the desk, they sometimes do not make an effort on their own. While requesting assistance at the desk could be one of the lessons to be learned, it can lead to much repetitive and time consuming instruction at the desk. Any skills program will increase the load on the desk because it will create more astute students who have learned the value of the reference librarian.

Slide presentations with discussion sessions or class presentations with assignments are other possibilities. One school printed the instructional material in its daily student newspaper.[26] The class presentations will have to be planned with accompanying visual materials, assignments, grading, and evaluation. Where many sessions are planned, scheduling can be a problem as well as obtaining the cooperation of librarians in making the presentations.

Computer assisted instruction (CAI) may be used either for a class or for student workshops, though it requires the availability of equipment and maintenance. With equipment proliferating rapidly, students may be faced with a further problem of knowing which computer terminal to use for which purpose. The initial preparation of a computer course can be lengthy, but probably not more than for other courses when they are initially planned. Preparation of CAI may require the assistance of a programmer. An advantage of CAI is the ability to keep track of individual students' progress and to keep statistics.

If a librarian is instituting a new program or looking for ways of changing an existing program, ideas for ways in which to teach library skills can be found in the library literature or in clearinghouse materials.[27] Materials can be requested from specific schools once programs are identified. Examples of workbooks and exercises can be obtained and adapted to the local situation.

Designing courses and teaching library research is a greater challenge to the bibliographic instructor because what is really being taught is problem solving and critical thinking.[28] In advanced courses, it is necessary to teach concepts rather than simply techniques. Librarians involved in the earlier years of the bibliographic movement studied the literature of the psychology of learning and education to work out methodologies for instruction.[29] Several publications have discussed the use of conceptual frameworks for instruction.[30] Other librarians have developed ways of teaching which require active participation on the part of the student.[31]

One of the tenets of bibliographic instruction is that it is best to teach the use of the library at the moment when the student needs to use the library, when what is being presented is practiced and learned by doing. This is one reason bibliographic classes and workshops always have endless numbers of exercises or assignments to be completed. The assignments are quite often designed around students' own work in a subject discipline.

It is but a simple step then to teaching subject oriented classes. Librarian subject specialists working closely with the faculty in their subject area may decide that a course would be advantageous at either the graduate or undergraduate level. Of course, no library can possibly afford to offer bibliographic courses in every discipline being taught at a university, but certainly courses of this nature can and should be offered. Science information sources, social sciences, chemistry, political science, business, speech and hearing, and music are only a few subject areas in which courses can be offered.

In addition to assignments, textbooks have been developed for research or subject bibliography classes. Actually, self-paced research workbooks have been developed in some subject fields similar to general skills workbooks. Some of these have been published, or as stated before can be found in collections at clearinghouses.[32] Subject courses may be viewed as bibliography classes in which the bibliography and access tools are presented with assignments to insure that the students learn to use the basic tools of the subject.

## IN-CLASS PRESENTATIONS

Evan Farber and William Kirk pioneered the methodologies for this type of instruction at Earlham College,[33] but librarians across the country have supplied this type of instruction for many years, working with faculty members for successful presentations. Faculty members may ask a librarian to show their students around the library. Most librarians take the opportunity to do much more by way of initiating students into the literature of the subject. As a reinforcement, the librarian may give students a printed handout so that they need not jot down titles and will have the list for consultation the next time they return to the library. Every institution will have departments that are more hospitable to library instruction than others.

Librarians arrange with faculty members to make a presentation at the beginning of an in-depth research project with an exercise designed to assist the students in their projects. Occasionally these sessions are scheduled when the professor will be presenting a paper or attending a professional meeting somewhere else. In these cases, the purpose can be defeated by lack of attendance by the students because they sense that the faculty member does not consider the session important enough to attend, and they can safely cut class. The library can institute a policy requiring an instructor's presence for a library lecture.

As with orientation tours, forms can be used for requesting educational sessions in classes. Someone in the department will need to collect the requests and assign librarians to the sessions.

In-class instructional sessions can be great time savers for the reference staff because a number of students are shown the intricacies of specialized tools at the same time rather than individually at the desk. There is an added advantage if the presentations are given by the expert on the library staff because the teacher becomes the message. The students know which will be the best librarian to seek out for assistance.[34]

Presentations need to be well organized and based on subject matter which the students will find essential to the completion of the professor's assignment. Pertinent bibliographies or graphic displays of what is being conveyed should be prepared for student use after the presentation. The information shown will only be valuable if it is thoroughly explained in the presentation.

If the presentations are repeated year after year, the library might consider developing a slide tape show or video. Slide programs have the advantage of being reasonably easy to update, although since the slides are cued to the audio tape, it isn't always as easy as simply replacing slides. Slide shows can turn into a nightmare if the cues of the tape slip out of synchronization with the slides. Fortunately equipment has been improved and cassettes have been substituted for reel to reel tapes, somewhat alleviating problems.[35] Videos present less of a problem in terms of machinery since the use of cassettes has become widespread.

There are quite a number of commercially available slide tape shows which can be used for instructional sessions. Before these shows are purchased or borrowed, they must be evaluated either by previewing them or reading reviews.[36]

There are a lot of dull slide tape shows in existence. It helps to base the presentations on subjects of current interest to the students. While the Los Angeles riots (1965 and 1992) or the Oakland, California, fire (1991) were good topics when they occurred, after a year or two it was time for some other topics to be chosen.

To introduce online searching and CD-ROM, it is essential that librarians make use of liquid crystal display units designed to project computer screens. There are several available for purchase. While overhead projector transparencies can be used, they are not as dynamic or as explanatory as interactive demonstrations. Ideally a classroom will have computer terminals for students to practice on while instruction is presented.

Making bibliographic instruction interesting to students is a problem. One solution has been to develop programs for active learning in which the students develop their own solutions to problems and thus become enthusiastic about solving the problems presented.

## Short Sessions

Various types of workshops can be offered by the library outside of any class; for example, sessions on use of the online catalogs or preparation of term papers. These workshops should be scheduled at various times during the day in order that all students who wish to attend will be able to. The programs need to be advertised and promoted.

In spite of the fact that online catalogs are designed to be user-friendly and feature help screens, as do many of the CD-ROM databases, demonstrations are effective in allowing the student to see firsthand how to use a database. Usually workshops can be combined with handout leaflets.

Term paper clinics have been instituted at a number of schools. Although what is taught can be extremely useful, in some cases a lot of publicity is needed to entice students to attend. The clinics can teach general search strategy, concepts and types of bibliographic tools, but it is difficult to make the information meaningful to all in attendance when the audience may contain everyone from religious studies majors to electrical engineers. Those who attend should be given the option of following up the clinic with individual consultations by appointment with subject specialists. Clinics can be set up for various subject areas or subjects.

Since in many cases students are not aware of reference service itself, they may be even less aware of the types of individual service available. While ideally every student when starting a research project or dissertation might benefit from a conference with a librarian, it would be impossible to offer such a service if all students took advantage of it.

Faculty library instruction falls into the category of short workshops. Because of the changes in access to library collections, faculty members need updates on the library from time to time.[37] These presentations will inform the faculty of what the library offers and how they can take advantage of the new technology and new services such as document delivery. Such sessions will assist them in their own research as well as making them aware that their students may need similar presentations. The library might share with a computer center the instruction of faculty in the use of networks.

These presentations to the faculty are a good opportunity for the librarians to sell themselves as professionals and not mere technicians. It may not be necessary to claim as Holler does that information retrieval is a full-fledged discipline, but it should be recognized as a complex intellectual task.[38]

*Chapter 13.*

# Publications and Exhibits

Today it is essential for reference librarians to produce publications as an alternative means of assisting their patrons. Students need these in order to use the library on their own without instruction or reference service, particularly when service is not available. Many students like the ability these publications give them to make use of information sources on their own. Reference librarians can use them as well in assisting patrons, knowing that the publications can provide students with enough information to proceed on their own.

Libraries have always put out publications, ranging from beautifully printed and illustrated guides to mimeographed notices of hours or loan policies. In fact, in the previous chapter on instruction, it was suggested that at least informal publications be issued in a number of instances.

In most cases, publications are the direct result of libraries' identifying a need for them. Publications inform and instruct patrons. They offer a highly acceptable alternative to other means of instruction in an academic community where patrons wish to be self-sufficient and learn on their own.

Not all publications will emanate solely from the reference department, but since the reference librarians are most closely involved with patrons it is usually they who discover the need for a publication and work out ways of satisfying the need. Most libraries have a policy for issuing publications as well as procedures for having them accepted and issued. Acceptable formats may be determined and designed for various types of publications. The library needs to decide who will design and produce them. They can be prepared in-house, by other units on campus or by commercial printers.

At most schools, a guide to the libraries on campus is produced, telling all the pertinent facts about them and perhaps including photographs and floor plans. Besides informing the patron, the guide functions as a public relations tool. A spinoff from the guides is a printed walking tour used for orientation purposes. Printed walking tours give much the same information as the guides, but are designed to be read while walking through the library. There can also be guides to special units in a library such as a special collections room or a map room. As library guides are often substantial and expensive to print, simple fact sheets (including statistics) are sometimes prepared as well for public relations purposes.

Other types of publications can be developed for specific needs. Usually a librarian will figure out, after explaining the same information ten times in a row, that a simple leaflet can give the same information.

The first kind of leaflet that comes to mind, in a library of any significant size, is one giving the location of call numbers. Most large university libraries and some smaller ones have multiple stacks or floors (in some, there are more stacks than floors). The student will need to be informed on which floor various classes of material can be found. This publication may be duplicated in posters throughout the library and as part of floor plan handouts. Since librarians in the Circulation Department or Stack Services Department are more concerned about floor location than those in the Reference Department, and more likely to know immediately when there are changes in location, they may be the ones to create this publication.

Leaflets explaining how to use the catalog (card or online), how to find journal articles (an infinitely repetitive question at a reference desk), or how to find book reviews and biographical data are other possibilities.[1] When students approach the desk with assignments, they can be handed a leaflet—with, of course, an invitation to return to the desk if help is still needed.

When patrons begin to use an online catalog at remote locations through networking, the library needs to issue a leaflet quickly to provide the user with information on connecting to the database, including the search commands.[2] Where an online catalog is provided, search commands probably deserve a leaflet for use in the library. Many libraries find it useful to have flip charts next to the online catalog, rather than leaflets, to assist patrons.

Subject lists of databases that are available in the library on CD-ROM can also be of value. Reference librarians can use the subject list to mark the CD-ROMs which might be of use for a student's topic. Individual leaflets on each of these databases or covering several as grouped by protocols used (for example, Silver Platter or Wilson) are useful at the point where the CDs are used.

In these cases, leaflets are called point-of-use publications in the library literature. Library publications and commercially prepared publications have been used at point of use for printed bibliographic tools as well. In some cases, these have been tacked into the front of volumes; elsewhere they may be flip charts. In fact, a good many leaflets could be called point-of-use aids although they may be available in a central location rather than next to the tool.

These leaflet publications are best made brief and should feature headings that quickly identify for the student the information he might need. They can be standard 8½ by 11 inch size but are easier to use if folded in half, either vertically or horizontally. Publications can even be punched for collecting in a notebook. Vertical leaflets can be tucked into books or notebooks. The narrow format militates against long explanations that might be possible in bigger formats, but brief explanations or identifications of terms are easier for the patron to grasp quickly. What is needed is something that can be glanced through in a very few minutes with the salient points easy to refer back to.

In addition to issuing a brief publication, libraries may wish to put out a larger publication with fuller explanations of the same topics. The larger publication provides the complete information that patrons may desire, and the leaflet may be kept on hand for quick reference.

Publications should be attractive, perhaps colorful. They can be standardized in appearance and typeface, being designed by one person, or each can be produced as librarians see fit. Accordion pleated brochures have been used as well as ones with pages of decreasing size so that the edge provides the index. They can even be offered in a series and numbered. They should be inexpensive to produce, for it is difficult to prevent their being used as scratch paper from time to time. To discourage such use, large areas of white space should not be part of their design. Examples which can be used as a basis for developing in-house publications are available in instructional clearinghouses or can be picked up when visiting another library. Sometimes they are displayed at conferences or workshops.

In the discussion of instruction, handouts were mentioned. These can be merely typed lists of materials (mini-guides to the literature or short bibliographies) that are either produced on the computer or cut and pasted when updated, then retyped or copied. Guides to the literature, when used repeatedly, can be printed and made available for any user in addition to being passed out in classes. Prepared by the subject specialists, they can be very effective.

Topical bibliographies, covering for example the Los Angeles riots or the Gulf War are of interest to the users of a library and are fun to prepare. They often save time in answering repeated questions on their particular topics, but are time consuming to prepare. The decision to produce them will be based on the priorities of the department or the enthusiasm of one librarian.

Librarians can benefit from having patrons tell them what they like and don't like about the publications and how helpful they have been, but this information is difficult to obtain. The best feedback on the success of a publication is its continually being picked up and used.

## Exhibits

As with some of the other ways in which the patrons are assisted in the library, exhibits are not necessarily the realm of the reference departments although they quite often end up a reference department responsibility. Other departments such as Special Collections may instead be responsible for exhibits or share the responsibility with the reference department.

Equipment for exhibits can be a limiting factor. A library may have any of several types of exhibit cases—flat cases, upright cases, or a combination of types—or may have none at all. A library that does put on exhibits needs some sort of policy as to what is appropriate to be shown in these cases.

Exhibits may be used strictly for instruction, but more often they are used to inform patrons of special materials in the library or to display materials from the library that are closely related to some event on campus or in the world. They can display winners of book contests or books that have meant something to a faculty member. The possibilities are endless.[3]

If the reference department is responsible for the displays, one person will have to take on the responsibility for scheduling the exhibits, setting them up and advertising them. Forms can be used for submission of requests for exhibits, much as suggested earlier for orientation programs.

# Chapter 14.

# Evaluation

No discussion of reference work in the academic library would be complete without considering the topic of evaluation. Evaluation is an integral part of the management of reference departments. For individual programs such as instructional sessions it is particularly clear that an evaluation should be planned as part of their development to ascertain their success. The goals and objectives of a program are determined, activities are designed to achieve the objectives, and an evaluation takes place to determine whether the aims of the programs have been met.

It is perhaps less obvious that an evaluation of regular desk service needs to take place. But librarians should not smugly assume that they are doing the best possible job for the students. An evaluation helps them verify their successes and identify areas for improvement.

The library profession has recognized the need for measurement and evaluation of its services for many years. At the beginning and often even now, efforts aimed toward quantitative measures of service. More recently, interest has shifted toward the qualitative evaluation of services.[1]

Not only have the results of studies in evaluation been published, but from time to time, articles have appeared which review these studies.[2] Von Seggern states, "Only a very small portion of the available literature on this topic [about 60 citations] is presented here as a potential starting point for the assessment of reference services."[3] Murfin states that from 1976 to 1982 there were 238 publications on assessment of reference service.[4] The outpouring did not abate in the eighties. It is not the intention here to review the literature once again, but to indicate why evaluation is important, what can be evaluated and how evaluations have taken place.

For both desk service and special service programs, administrators need evaluative information for management decisions on a librarywide level. Librarians on the front line of service in a reference department need to know how effective their service is in order to insure its continued high quality and to identify ways in which service might be improved.

It is in the realm of decision-making that evaluation has its major importance for administrators. As Baker states, evaluation "should be thought of as a management tool whose main purposes are to identify current strengths, limitations, and failures, and to suggest ways to improve service."[5]

Thus, library administrators not only must prove the worth of library service programs from time to time, but must have available the evaluative information on which to base decisions.[6] As accountable administrators, they must justify the expenditure of funds for service in terms of its value to users.

Runyon has suggested five major data needs for administrators: (1) measures of the effects of policy, procedural, and organizational changes; (2) supporting data for budget requests to funding authorities and allocation of funds between library departments; (3) feedback data on patron behavior; (4) historical data for analysis of changes within a single library over time and for comparative analysis with other libraries; and (5) internal data communication, or communication between the reference librarian and the administrator.[7]

For their purposes, administrators like to have measurable quantities. While statistics can be of use to administrators, it is difficult to identify the quality of the service programs and their value to users in terms of numbers.[8] Yet both quantitative measurements and qualitative assessments can be used in the evaluation of reference services.

The whole reference program as well as the steps of the reference transaction can be examined to determine what parts need thorough evaluation or improvement. Then, evaluative instruments can be developed to examine various features, making use of studies that have already been performed elsewhere. In fact, in reading about the results of a study, it is sometimes possible to apply the lessons learned without having to perform a new study. Various types of studies will be discussed at the end of this section.

## *Inputs*

Librarians have found it useful to evaluate their work in terms of inputs and outputs. In ratings for accreditations of libraries and for comparison with other libraries, evaluators have mostly been concerned with input measures which can be readily ascertained. For reference services, input measures may include the size and excellence of the collection, the organization and availability of services, factors relating to the size of the staff, and the extensiveness of the education and training of librarians.[9]

Size of a collection can be important since in some studies of libraries with large collections, librarians are shown to do a better job than those who work with small collections.[10] There appears to be a correlation between the number of reference transactions and the size of the reference collection.[11] In spite of studies that have been done, it is difficult to determine the optimum size of a collection for a particular library. Increasing the size of the collection may increase the ability of librarians to find answers to questions, but this depends to some extent on the original size of the collection.[12]

The quality of collections can be determined by comparison with standard lists of reference books. The availability of titles in a few subject areas can be examined as a reflection of the whole collection. The collection can be checked for currency of titles by comparing citations either of outstanding examples of reference materials or of those reviewed in library journals and serials.[13]

Availability and organization of services embrace such factors as location of the desk, hours open, staffing, provision of an information desk, quality of the staff, layout of reference materials, and appearance or aura of the reference areas.[14] In evaluating reference service, all of these things must be considered. Some of them have been discussed previously. The amount of time per week that the library and service points are open affects at least the quantity of users served, since the more hours the desk is staffed the greater the number of transactions.[15] As discussed previously, quality of access to the collection through the catalog and other devices helps insure that reference librarians can give quality services.

The size of the reference staff and their deployment undoubtedly affects the quality of service. The experience, skills, and personal attributes and attitudes of the reference librarians can affect service. A careful recruitment program should insure a quality staff. Librarians' library school training and advanced degrees beyond their library degree can indicate a more knowledgeable staff and an understanding of the research process which will make it possible for them to assist the students with their research problems.

## Quantitative Measurements

Quantitative measurements of reference transactions are important for library administrators and for heads of reference services. Besides desk statistics, such statistics as the number of orientation and instructional sessions presented, the number who take part in them, the number of leaflets prepared, the number of online searches conducted, and the number of interlibrary loan requests processed are valuable figures for determining workload and resultant staffing needs. The statistics can verify the quantitative success of programs and imply their usefulness.

In order to identify useful quantitative measures and provide for consistency in data collection, the library profession has been concerned, both for public and academic libraries, with establishing standards for data collection for the whole library as well as for reference so that comparisons can be made.[16] Both standards and clear definitions of directional, informational, ready reference and research questions are necessary for the sake of consistency in the reporting of statistics to the profession and to insure that the data collected can be of use.[17]

At a reference desk some of the characteristics of the questions which are asked can be considered input measures. These characteristics can be measured in a great number of ways: total questions, who asks them, subject of questions, type of questions, sources used to answer them. Some outputs such as accuracy of response, length of time of the transaction, sources used, and referrals made can also be subject to quantitative measurement.

Librarians have kept statistics of transactions for many years, usually by making hatch marks on a calendar or on data sheets with some classification of questions. While perhaps useful for roughly identifying busy times of the day, these statistics are rarely accurate. When librarians are not busy, they may forget to mark the calendar. If they are very busy, they do not have time to mark it. Once librarians realize they have not marked any transactions down, they mark the calendar later, during a lull. These hatch marks usually reflect subjective impressions of how busy they were rather than an accurate count.[18]

Daily hatch marks provide gross statistics on total desk activity, but perhaps more importantly they identify busy times of the day—information of great value in determining the desk schedule. In one study, it was found that reference desk statistics correlate with operating hours and the number of persons in the library (turnstile count).[19]

Much statistical information can be provided by sampling, particularly if a baseline of totals from the hatching of previous years is available. Times for sampling can be determined by turnstile count by the week in the quarter or semester, or as indicated by high, medium and low usage.[20] With the burden of keeping statistics spread over a brief period of time, librarians may be motivated to make a more accurate count than when they record transactions on an ongoing basis.

The number of transactions at a reference desk can be a useful statistic, but to produce more useful data, other information can be recorded. Some libraries have categorized the count of questions into directional or informational, brief reference or extended reference.[21] Questions have been categorized by length of time spent on them, number of steps taken to find the answer,[22] or by subject. Subject classification of questions may be particularly useful for collection development or determining whether a subject specialist is needed. Very elaborate forms have been developed to yield information about success and failure of transactions.[23]

National and state reporting requirements will influence data collection activities, particularly in public institutions. Transaction logs and statistical packages have made it possible to gather information on who uses electronic services, what databases they use and how frequently, how they construct search strategies, and what results ensue.

The use to be made of the statistics will determine which statistics will be kept and how reference transactions will be recorded. This is another way of saying that the goal and objective for the measurement must be determined before any measurement takes place.

## *Accuracy*

Since the early seventies, one goal has been to determine the accuracy of answers. When complete and correct answers proved, in a number of studies, to have been found only in the neighborhood of 50 percent the library profession viewed the situation as a crisis.[24] But in the process of investigating accuracy and what to do about it, librarians found that if they merely asked patrons whether their questions were answered, 75 percent said yes.[25]

Accuracy perhaps has more relevance to public libraries, for much of the assistance given in public libraries consists of help in finding facts. Academic reference librarians serve a different function, primarily that of assisting and instructing students in finding material for their course work. For the academic library, factual questions represent a very small portion of the help requested.[26]

To use studies of accuracy in academic libraries, librarians are letting this small fraction of the desk activities which are measurable represent all of reference service.[27] As part of the analysis of accuracy, the studies were interested in whether referrals were made appropriately.

Efforts to determine why questions were not answered correctly turned up a number of possibilities: a requested work was not owned by the library, the librarian did not know the source, the librarian did not know how to use the source, or the librarian did not understand the question, among others. Knowledge of reasons for failures could point to areas for training so as to improve service.

## Statistics for Other Programs

Statistics on reference programs other than the desk can be used in planning. For example, if a library instruction course has an enrollment of fewer than ten, and takes one-fourth of one librarian's time in a quarter or semester, the administration might consider dropping it. When tours or instructional sessions have only a handful of students, perhaps they should be dropped or shifted to another time when more students might attend. If orientation tours and instructional sessions have too many students who attend, the groups can be split or a session can be scheduled at another time. In order to provide for the possibility of splitting a tour group, for example, personnel must be scheduled for backup.

## Need for Qualitative Analysis

Quantitative analysis does have a role to play in the evaluation of academic libraries, but for the head of reference and the individual reference librarian to insure the effectiveness of their services, they need qualitative evaluation of their success in providing for the information needs of the user.[28]

Reference librarians will want to know whether the users' needs are satisfied, whether the users obtain the information requested, whether the information given is accurate, and whether the librarians assisted and instructed the users in such a way that the user can help himself.[29] In an effort to give the best possible service, reference librarians will want to pinpoint problems so they can be solved.[30]

In order to evaluate departmental effectiveness and individual performance, it is necessary to determine what the department wants to know before deciding how to design an analytical system for providing the information. In a recent article, Hernon, a librarian who along with McClure has spent the most time and effort on evaluation of reference, uses the term "utility measures" to remind librarians that the evaluation must have a purpose for improvement or decision-making. The design of an instrument must be based on the goal of the evaluation; i.e., what exactly the study is trying to accomplish—to prove worth, serve as a basis for improving service, or to provide performance evaluation?[31]

Reference librarians want to know how well the department as a whole is performing as well as how effective the individual librarian is in order to develop ways of improving service. Primarily the concern of the profession has been the evaluation of the reference transaction and consequently individual performance. The reference transaction has been seen to be a complex act made up of a number of factors: behavioral aspects, knowledge of sources, reference skills. These factors can be studied in various ways.

## KNOWLEDGE OF SOURCES AND SEARCH STRATEGY

Knowledge of reference sources and ability to use them can be measured by written tests. Skills in search strategy can be determined by posing written reference problems to be solved as a test. Ability to use online facilities can also be tested. Tests for accuracy can be administered in written form. While tests for knowledge are rarely given after library school, many of the accuracy studies are performance tests.

## BEHAVIORAL ASPECTS

The behavioral aspects of the reference transaction which are not subject to quantitative analysis will need to be evaluated. Establishing behavioral standards and competencies and how they are indicated would appear to be a requisite for evaluating desk performance.[32]

## Methods of Qualitative Analysis

Statistical analysis and qualitative judgments of performance can be undertaken in a variety of ways. Techniques that have been used include observations, interviews, and surveys of various types.

### OBSERVATIONS

Observations can be performed obtrusively by professional observers, by using an audio recorder, by making a video recording, or by administering questions. Performance observations can be made by outside evaluators, heads of departments or peers.[33] For any of these observations, forms with desired behaviors can be prepared and librarians rated on a scale for each item by peers or department heads. Behavioral standards and competencies and how they are indicated for most evaluations are useful for peer evaluations or for observations by department heads. In considering individual performance, standards provide a basis for comparison and for identifying improvement needs. (See discussion of standards, p. 78–81.)

Some librarians find peer evaluation threatening, but some have found the evaluations valuable in pinpointing areas in which they need improvement. Peer evaluations can improve departmental performance and enhance departmental morale.

The work of individual librarians is often evaluated for merit increases and promotions. These evaluations need to be based on clearly stated expectations. While evaluations occur once a year or every two or three years, heads of reference departments should have ongoing discussions with librarians in which they can suggest improvements or offer commendation.

It is difficult for an evaluator to observe activity at a desk and to note and record all the nuances of what goes on. It is far better to make audio or video tapes of the interviews. Lynch's taped interviews in a study reported in 1978 showed how taping can provide information on the interview and be used as an evaluative tool as well.[34] While audio tapes are useful, video tapes can capture more of the transaction because they show the nonverbal cues which are missing from audio tapes.[35] In either audio or video taping, care must be taken to make sure that the privacy of the patron and confidentiality of his question are maintained.

Videos can be rerun any number of times. When they are first viewed, the librarians who were filmed can explain their thought processes or frame of mind during the interview as well as the rationale for questions and use of nonverbal communication.[36] Jennerich feels that in using video techniques only one or two aspects of an interview should be observed and worked on for improvement at a time, such as use of eye contact. Observers can then concentrate on that aspect and work to improve it.[37]

Both obtrusive and unobtrusive methodologies have been used. In obtrusive testing the librarians know they are being tested, so in some cases they may affect the results by doing a much better job than they ordinarily do, knowing they are observed or tested. In fact, it has been suggested that librarians should treat every question asked by patrons as if it were an obtrusive test. The use of recording devices makes the observations obtrusive. Yet, in the case of audio and video taping, librarians sometimes forget that they are being observed and simply act naturally.

Unobtrusive testing makes use of a group of questions drawn up and usually presented to service departments by persons hired to behave like patrons, either in the library or on the telephone. In addition to determining the accuracy of the answers, the surrogate patrons may also note whether a source is given for the answer and perhaps something about the librarians giving the service such as the perceived attitude of the librarian in terms of helpfulness and approachability.[38] In designing studies of this nature care must be given to the validity of the reference questions used. They may be based on actual questions previously asked or developed and tested for the unobtrusive study.[39]

## INTERVIEW

Patrons can be interviewed either after a reference transaction for evaluation of the particular instance or at other times to learn needs, attitudes, and perhaps specific criticisms. One university successfully used focus group interviews to receive feedback on services.[40] Interviews or focus group sessions can be taped so that an analysis of them can take place later.

## SURVEYS

Surveys are another obtrusive measure used for evaluation. Both librarians and patrons can be asked to fill out questionnaires after a reference encounter, or they can both be queried by surveyors. A system for matching the forms for a single encounter needs to be part of the design of the survey.[41] As with other evaluations, a clear idea of the information desired must be considered in developing the questions in the survey.

Surveys sampling both users and non-users have been distributed to find out about student attitudes and use of a library. Most user surveys indicate that patrons of reference services are very satisfied with the service even when they have not received complete or accurate answers to their questions. In one study, patrons indicated greater satisfaction with the service than the estimate of the librarians on the same encounter.[42]

As has been noted, there are numerous ways of evaluating desk performance. In deciding on which evaluative methodology to use, librarians must have a clear idea of the objectives of the study so that the method provides information for improvement of service. Quantitative measures are best for justification of a service; qualitative determination for analysis and improvement. For qualitative analysis, reference transaction observation (directly or by using audio or video tapes) would appear to be the most effective means.[43]

## *Evaluation of Special Programs*

Particularly for specific programs such as bibliographic instruction, evaluation is an essential part of program development. The objectives are determined before the program is implemented and an evaluation is made to determine whether the objectives have been met.

In the case of bibliographic instruction a whole literature on evaluation has grown up[44] and continues to be enlarged[45] Various methodologies have been developed. Surveys are useful since they can be handed out at the end of instructional sessions. They can have multiple choice answers on a scale such as one to five. Surveys can be developed in cooperation with campus agencies for improvement of instruction. They can be machine graded with correlations made between the various questions using a statistical package (such as the Statistical Package for the Social Sciences).

Open-ended questions where students write narrative evaluations take more time to analyze. When they were used at USCB, reactions to the library's courses were very positive, but they did not provide the kind of information needed to improve or redesign the program. Since written surveys basically indicate attitudes, they document affective learning. In most cases, library instruction has been shown to eliminate library anxiety, the original fearfulness of the student, replacing it with the confidence of at least knowing where to begin.

Many universities have successfully used pre- and post-course tests to assess learning. Efforts have even been made to determine the effect of library instruction on students' course work in other subjects, though these effects are much more difficult to ascertain and must be gauged by such indicators as students' grades or the extent or quality of their bibliographies for term projects. It is still more difficult to work out a means of testing students at the end of their college careers to determine the lasting effect of library instruction.

Orientation and instruction sessions can be evaluated more easily than leaflets or brochures because there is a captive audience. Evaluation forms in brochures are usually discarded rather than turned in. The best indication of the value of leaflets or brochures is their continual use. Of course, some patrons will verbally praise or analyze a publication.

Since publications are impersonal they are less likely to prompt the kind of feedback sometimes given to the reference librarian: "Thank you for helping me. I found just what I needed." Occasionally librarians have received written commendation on help given or on an instructional session. Boxes of candy or flowers have been sent as thank-yous to the department. Librarians are delighted that someone out there cares.

Suggestion boxes sometimes elicit complimentary comments by patrons although they are more apt to indicate criticism. While not a formal means of evaluation, unsolicited positive comments are influential in persuading reference librarians to keep up the good work.

## Improvement

One of the major purposes of developing an evaluative instrument to assess some portion of reference service is the improvement of that service.[46] While evaluation is useful to library administrations for justification and decision making, unless it is also used to identify the status of service and identify problem areas for the development of methods for improvement of service, it is an empty exercise. As Young states the need for improvement, "The far more difficult question of remedial action lies before us."[47]

Librarians are constantly working to improve the quality of their service. They recognize that they need not only to know new sources and skills, but to refresh their memories about old ones and monitor their own behavior. Even if they do not make elaborate evaluations, librarians have always worked out numerous ways in which they hope to improve reference services.

It seems obvious, but the first way to insure improvement of reference service is to have good library management. Good managers will determine activities that satisfy users' needs. They will promote the morale of the staff by creating a team. They will seek ways to motivate the staff to perform well and to seek improvement. They will develop goals and objectives and devise ways to carry them out. Only by having clearly stated objectives can a reference manager work to promote desired characteristics.[48] For the desk service, objectives might take the form of behavioral standards and policies for the reference transaction.

How can a library insure good management? First, persons with ability should be hired. Then, adequate training must be given when they begin their duties.[49] The training can be given in the library, on campus or in outside courses and workshops. Watching good managers in a library, it may appear that managers are born rather than made, but some sort of managerial training can be useful if only to make managers aware of what constitutes good management.

Managers do have a heavy load in identifying problems and in working out solutions for the physical environment, collection, programs, projects and priorities. By studying and analyzing these elements, reference managers will find solutions to try and then to evaluate. From evaluations of individual programs, they will decide whether they need to be redesigned or given a different priority.

In regard to personnel, reference managers must determine whether the problems identified can be solved by rescheduling, job enlargement, retraining, continuing education or if necessary perhaps reassignment. They will work on methods for improving performance of the staff.

In developing a model for staff development, Weaver-Meyers suggests that there are two types of learning experiences for the staff: staff development and continuing education.[50] She suggests that staff development is the concern of the library and continuing education is the province of the individual librarian. In practice the two overlap, for practically any continuing education program will develop the individual staff member for better service.[51] Reference managers will hold in-house training sessions, encourage attendance at conferences, workshops, and classes, and provide the opportunity for professional reading.

To eliminate the errors in reference service that have been shown to exist, both by the profession and by local evaluation, and to provide actively for the needs of patrons, libraries must not only analyze what they are doing and determine how errors are made, but must use some of the ways discussed to improve service to their patrons.

## Chapter 15.

# Management

Management is the planning, organizing, directing and decision-making in library activities designed to satisfy the mission and goals of the academic library. All reference librarians are involved in the management of the library to the extent that they are responsible for their own activities and the programs which they have been assigned, most of which have been discussed: instruction, orientation, the reference collection, supervision of the information desk, training, computer searching, exhibits, publications, electronic databases and equipment, among others.

For their assignments, reference librarians may develop the policy and procedures for the activity, coordinate with fellow librarians or supervise those involved in the work, including library assistants and students. In their area, they are responsible for training and evaluating those they supervise. The authority which they have in executing their responsibilities depends to a great extent on the organizational structure of the library in which they work.

For librarians who supervise a number of people, or for heads or coordinators of a reference department, it is advantageous to have some training in management, if for no other reasons than the understanding it gives of one's own management style. Traditionally, the organizational structure in an academic library, and for the reference department as part of the organizational structure, has been hierarchical with close supervision down the line. In reference departments, this meant a head of reference responsible for the activities of the reference department, but reporting to and accountable to the library administration (i.e., the next person up the line, such as an assistant librarian in charge of public service or the director).

Recently, with the institution of the faculty status model, more collegial patterns have developed with the position of head of the reference department perhaps being rotated.[1] In fact, Smith suggests that the organization chart of the future will be a horizontal line.[2] One of the organizational recommendations of the task forces at the Rethinking Reference Institutes at both Berkeley and Duke was to flatten the hierarchy.[3]

It would appear that in an absolutely flattened organization, either every reference librarian would feel responsible for everything as they do when they care about the service of the department as a whole, or no one would feel responsible for anything. Ideally, librarians feel responsible for their own assignment in the department or the library.

Even in hierarchies, there are differences in management styles.[4] Decisions may be made at the highest level with directives proceeding down the line. Usually, this command style is tempered by consultation. In consultative patterns, advice is sought, and the person in charge makes the final decision. In the collaborative style, the head agrees to go along with group recommendations if certain conditions are met. The consensus style is one in which consensus must be reached before something is implemented. Consensus is not compromise, but something all can agree on. In the last configuration, the reference department as a whole determines goals and objectives for the department and methods of carrying them out.

Under an authoritative department head, reference librarians have often been unhappy, feeling that they had no effective input in the running of their department. They may be more upset when their advice is sought in written form but never seems to be accepted or implemented. Most reference librarians probably would rather have the head of the department function as a coordinator so that it would be possible to thrash out problems in an open meeting and have the chair accept a consensus.

In some hierarchies, reference librarians are free to develop their own ideas and programs with the understanding that someone up the line may stop them.[5] This approach allows for creativity, but falls short in the area of overall planning and coordination. A more collegial structure has been achieved by splitting up the responsibilities of the reference department, either with or without a head of the department.

For personnel matters, which loom as a major responsibility for those in charge of reference departments, it seems advantageous to have one person as overall director of the department. One person can insure that personnel matters are efficiently managed and can work for good morale and teamwork in the department. Through enthusiasm and care, department heads can motivate those that work with them. A head can determine assignments on the basis of the abilities or experience of the librarians. Major assignments should be made to the ablest. Where release of staff members is difficult because of library personnel guidelines, some department heads may identify members who can be given only minimal responsibilities with carefully determined procedures. Minimally capable members of departments make difficulties for the heads of departments in making assignments and for the library. These members cannot simply be assigned more hours on the desk because they will be minimally effective there as well.[6]

Heads can watch out that the most capable members of the department are not overloaded with responsibilities so that they begin to suffer what is called "burnout" in the current literature. When reference librarians lose the ability to operate at their best (or at all, in some cases), they are considered to have "burnout." Their time is too fractured, they have too much responsibility, and they are not taking enough time away from their work. They may even devote their off hours to library projects. An extensive literature has developed on the subject of librarian burnout.[7]

While heads may not necessarily hire or fire the librarians in their department, even though they might like to, they need to have the major input on these matters for the coordination of assignments and to ensure that capable persons with whom they can easily develop rapport are added to the department. Committees may examine qualifications of candidates and recommend who will be interviewed; later they may recommend which candidates, in what order, should be offered the position. Other librarians in the library may make recommendations. Also, the final selection may be made by the administration rather than the head of the department.

Regardless of who makes the decision, firing can be more difficult than hiring. The person reviewing a librarian's work must document carefully any deficiencies within the realm of what is feasible for firing in a given situation. Any tenure system needs to be taken into account, as does the existence of any committee that reviews the recommendations.

It is better to have a head of the department so that someone can take charge of the periodic reviews of the reference staff for retention or promotion. A department head may only coordinate the activities of those evaluating various parts of a librarian's assignment, rather than write the whole evaluation herself. Also, by discussing the work with the person being evaluated, a department head can commend outstanding work as well as discuss shortcomings and needs for improvement. It is for these discussions that standards can be of special value.

Heads may also counsel librarians on their career development path, especially when service to the library as a whole, the campus and the profession is considered to be an essential element of performing well on the job. Heads will counsel their staff in obtaining additional training or instruction when necessary.

Occasionally, heads become "other mothers" in making sure their staff members receive the attention they need for their health and welfare and in assisting them in solving problems in their private lives, if only by recommending they see trained professionals either on or off the campus.

Communication is a major factor in the management of libraries. Information must be exchanged within a department as well as with other librarians and the library administration. Meetings are a common place for communication to take place, but it may also take place through memos or e-mail. Even in libraries that do not emphasize a collegial management style, reference librarians attend a plethora of meetings. Kinds of meetings vary from library to library, but it is doubtful that any academic library does not have meetings. As part of their position, reference librarians attend some of these meetings. Which ones will to some extent be a matter of choice, but more often attendance will be determined by what is politic or required.

Some library systems have librarywide meetings once a year for librarians and staff, but probably not for all the student assistants since someone has to keep the library open while the meeting is in progress. Librarywide gatherings inform those who work in the library about programs, innovations and plans for the future, but mostly inform the staff about what the library administration wishes them to know. These sessions can often clear up rumors floating around by presenting the facts.

Reference librarians attend the public service divisional meetings and usually those for collection development librarians as well. The public service meetings assist the library in keeping consistency of service in various units. Collection development meetings may be broken down into subject groupings: social sciences, sciences and engineering, humanities. These smaller meetings are similar to the all-library meetings in informing librarians or librarians and staff about policies and procedures that are new or have been changed. A smaller group of collection development librarians or the librarian in charge of collection development may determine items for discussion or presentation at these subject meetings, but agenda items can be suggested by attendees prior to the meetings as well. There may be some discussion at these divisional gatherings, but more often these are informational or training meetings.

At the next level of meetings are departmental gatherings. The nature and frequency of these meetings depend to a great extent on the number of staff members in the department. Large meetings of the total reference staff are quite often for announcements—for example, reports of department heads' meetings which the department head attended. Yet it is important to have some discussion of departmental problems with the whole staff, including library assistants. Library assistants can make useful suggestions, particularly in regard to their own responsibilities. Without full departmental meetings, it is more difficult to develop departmental esprit de corps.

Meetings of just the reference librarians (without library assistants) are usually discussions of policy, methodology or program. Even for these meetings, however, input from all librarians may be solicited prior to the meeting and discussion kept to answering questions because of the difficulties of carrying on a discussion with more than five persons.[8] The head of a department may share the comments they have received with the whole department and open up the discussion rather than just reporting decisions based on the comments. Running a large meeting is a management skill that can be learned. There are books, videos, and consultants dealing with this kind of training.

In libraries with large reference staffs, there may be a smaller group which meets with the head of the department to discuss reference department decisions. Membership in this group may be automatically determined, consisting for example of unit heads or those in charge of various activities, or it may rotate or be made up of senior staff members. Those not in the small group may feel their thoughts and ideas are as worthy as those in the smaller group and want to participate more fully. Yet small groups may be the only way to accomplish some reference business.

In addition to a small administrative group within the department, task forces of two or more members may be set up to determine programs, changes, policies or solutions to problems. The department head will generally set the task force's mission, although the reference department as a whole may do so. How the task force operates depends to a great extent on the authority of the department head in running the department and on who has the responsibility for implementing the decisions.

Reference librarians need to meet regularly for training sessions. The preparation of these meetings may be the responsibility of one librarian with others taking part in the presentations or planning.

A new librarian should determine the management structure of the library, either when he interviews for a position or when he arrives on the job. From this discussion, it will be apparent that reference librarians in the future will need to be managers—of their own time, of programs, and of their library as a whole, probably working collegially with their fellow librarians.

# PART IV.

# Professional Responsibilities

This last section gives an overview of the whole nature of the professional reference librarian, from necessary personal characteristics to the kinds of general and specifically professional education that the reference librarian should have. Reference librarians cannot be fully effective as professionals for several years. Their first experiences as well as their in-house training can affect their ability to perform on the job. But before librarians can start work on a desk, they must obtain a position, which can be a trying proposition requiring knowledge of where to find openings and an understanding of the process by which librarians are hired.

As professionals, reference librarians have responsibilities to their library and to the profession which are not in evidence when they begin a position and which will not appear to be part of their job. Libraries can take some responsibility in initiating the new librarian to the whole range of possibilities: membership and official responsibilities in professional organizations, publication, the creation of workshops, and service to the school and community in which they live.

*Chapter 16.*

# Qualifications

Attributes of the reference librarian can be broken down into personality characteristics, qualities of mind, work habits and ability to work with others. Even though there is a consensus on personal qualities that are desirable, these qualities can exist in a wide variety of persons, so it is not the author's intention to describe one person or type of person. While reference librarian can mean extrovert, it does not have to. Librarians are usually bookish people who are happy with their own company. The shiest ones become technical process librarians, but assisting people requires only the ability to speak easily with whoever comes to the desk.

Reference librarians must have a genuine interest in and liking for people. They must be able to communicate effectively with both patrons and colleagues. The care and empathy which librarians have towards the feelings of the people they assist will be displayed in attentive behavior and active listening. Polite and courteous reference librarians will always appear friendly, approachable and helpful.

Librarians must be patient and tolerant in order to put up with student idiosyncrasies or possible unpleasantness. Personal or professional problems must be put aside while performing reference service. The student must experience nothing but pleasant assistance. Certainly a sense of humor can help librarian to keep smiling.

As service librarians, they will have a commitment to the satisfaction of the information needs of a wide variety of inquirers. Information needs in this context may simply be assistance in coping with the library system. While concern for the difficulties of the student can be feigned so that the student never knows, it is better that librarians really care about their inquiries. Librarians can become bored with repetitive questions, but if they focus on the joy of initiating the novice into intricacies of library use rather than on the similarity of requests, they may not find it a problem to answer the same need day after day.

Physical attributes consist of energy, tirelessness and stamina, or as Thomas put it, "marvelous feet."[1] It is impossible to be at peak performance every minute or for sustained periods of time. When the inability to operate at their best becomes endemic with reference librarians, the phenomenon of burnout discussed earlier has set in.[2]

Surprisingly enough, when listing four basic personal qualifications that library directors want, Patricia Battin does not mention the personal qualities discussed above (perhaps in part because she is not specifying reference librarians). However, her number one quality was "a first-rate mind with problem-solving abilities."[3] Certain qualities of the mind do make for a good reference librarian.

The present author's inclination is to look for nosiness, curiosity or inquisitiveness. Some colleagues have objected to the negative connotations of these words, but what is meant is simply a genuine interest in practically everything—people, ideas, information, methodologies. Granted, librarians may be more interested in some subjects than others; that is why they may specialize. But they need to have interests outside their specialty. An enthusiasm for new ideas, new methodologies, or new approaches to old problems is desirable, particularly at a time when reference librarians are actively reinventing their jobs.

Another qualification is a good memory. Neill has discussed various kinds of memory in his articles.[4] A librarian probably would do well to have all the kinds of memory he mentions. Especially crucial is memory of specific items and where to find them, or associational memory which identifies and sorts into the mental structure of the mind. Perhaps it could be said that the librarian's expertise rests on his ability to look things up, but without memory of types of sources, former use of them and ways of accessing information in a wide variety of sources, librarians would not be able to perform competently.

The ability to think of two things or even more at the same time, or to move rapidly from one subject to the next, can be useful. Probably most librarians do not realize that they have this ability even though they are masters of it. While a librarian is discussing with the student the information needed, he has already begun to figure out how to satisfy that need in his mind, or may be thinking of further possibilities for the last previous student if she should return. Thinking of more than one thing at a time does not preclude giving the student the attention he deserves.

It also helps to have a lively imagination, defined as "mental synthesis of new ideas from elements experienced separately."[5] Perhaps this is one element of what could be called problem solving. Perhaps what is meant by imagination for librarians is creativity. Certainly to meet the new challenges of the profession, librarians will need creativity and the flexibility to try innovative methods to solve unfamiliar problems. [6] In doing so they also need the quality of patience because they may not have instant success in having their ideas put into practice.

Battin also lists "concrete evidence of managerial abilities" as a needed quality.[7] This can be interpreted as it applies to work habits. Reference librarians should see the whole picture of service in the library as well as how they can fit into it. They should be self-starters who use their initiative in setting goals and determining plans for achieving them. They should be able to organize their own time, setting priorities so that their responsibilities are met in a timely fashion. In spite of seeing broad pictures, they should be attentive to details because they recognize that the whole framework of librarianship is based on the accuracy of specific information. They will be persistent in pursuing their objectives, always striving to improve their performance. The desire for improvement is the reason for evaluation and the basis for continuing education.

Management for reference librarians also means the ability to supervise others, either colleagues or library assistants. For colleagues, this may mean working cooperatively to accomplish goals. For library assistants this may mostly mean training them to operate on an optimal level. Because librarians need library assistants, they need to treat them with respect in what they ask them to do and how. It is the insecure librarian who is apt to lord it over the library assistant or to withdraw from sharing their expertise freely with their colleagues.

Traditionally reference departments have been full of prima donnas, those librarians who are particularly creative and self-directed. Actually reference librarians wouldn't be very good if they did not have those qualities to some degree, but the unfortunate consequence is that among the many different people individual librarians will have to work with, some will be harder to work with than others.

Reference librarians naturally hope to advance however they can. They must understand what it means to be a professional at the present time and that they may have to work with other librarians in reinventing their profession. Because some feel they must do this on their own, they may not be want to work with anyone else on questions or projects. Thus, reference librarians must be tactful in dealing with their colleagues. A beginning librarian will do well to secure a position in which teamwork and cooperation are emphasized.

*Chapter 17.*

# Education

## 1. General Education

Reference librarians need the best general education in college that they can afford. If they possess the mental characteristics already discussed, they will naturally tend to obtain a good education through pursuit of their wide interests. At the time the author went to college, many liberal arts schools required certain core courses in order to insure a good general education. After a swing to more specialization, colleges are now returning to such requirements, sometimes under the label of breadth requirements.

The results of a good education will be what D'Aniello discusses in terms of cultural literacy.[1] Cultural literacy should be the result of a good general education, but also the result of extensive reading. It is doubtful that anyone will become a librarian without having been a great reader. Since everything interests them, librarians will read anything and everything. It is no wonder that librarians are enthusiastic players of trivia games.

As part of this general education, prospective librarians should learn as many languages as feasible. Needless to say, it is also vital that they learn how to speak and write well in the English language.

## 2. Specialized Education

It is desirable for reference librarians working in a university or college environment to have taken advanced work in a specialized subject area. In some cases, work for a subject major may suffice, but advanced work for a master's or Ph.D. goes farther in giving librarians an understanding of the nature of academic research. Such specialized knowledge can make it possible for reference librarians to perform collection development duties, instruction and specialized tours in addition to serving as resource persons in the subject for the rest of the reference staff. Librarians with subject expertise become colleagues of faculty members just as they are with their library cohorts.

Subject specialization can add depth to the service in a reference department. Ideally, a library would like to have specialists in all subject fields. In reality, either some subjects fall through the cracks or librarians must take on either whole fields of knowledge (such as social sciences) or multiple subjects (such as sociology and economic or general history). Other librarians with subject expertise will end up in technical processing positions, or in some cases will have joint appointments in services. Occasionally subject specialists become bored with general questions, but ideally they will have sufficiently wide interests that this will not happen.

## 3. Library Education

To become a professional librarian it is usually necessary to complete a graduate degree in library sciences, information sciences or a similarly named discipline. (A master's degree is the basic requirement, although Ph.D.s are offered for those who wish to teach or who are interested in becoming administrators.) It is perhaps presumptuous to state what should be required for this formal education for librarianship with the existence of the King Report[2] which discusses competencies of librarians to be learned in library schools, but it seems reasonable to mention certain basic elements that the present author considers essential.

How to access information is the first thing that the reference librarian should learn in library school, since assistance in accessing the collection is the major role of the reference librarian.[3] This used to mean knowledge of the rules of entry for all types of materials in a card catalog, but now it goes beyond that to encompass an understanding of the format for entries in online catalogs, including information about fields and the use of tags to identify them.

More important than knowing how they are set up is the ability to use online catalogs and the online databases offered through vendors or on CD-ROM.[4] It may be more appropriate for librarians to learn general principles—when to use an online database over a printed tool, the existence of different search protocols for various databases rather than to memorize endless specifics that may change by the time they are working in a library. They do need to know about the technology of computers and networks and how they are used for access.

In learning to search online catalogs and databases, librarians will learn about the use of subject headings with controlled and uncontrolled vocabularies and about the use of thesauri when searching by controlled vocabularies. Although many databases offer keyword searching, searching by controlled vocabularies can be advantageous.

An understanding of the classification schemes such as Dewey and Library of Congress should be gained. Besides the schedule subject classification, it is important to understand where and when the schedule goes from general to specific and how cuttering is used throughout schedules for authors, subjects or geography.

Reference librarians obviously need to know about reference sources. While specific sources should be learned, it is perhaps more important to have structured knowledge of when to use specific types of sources and how to identify specific sources. This approach is valuable because, if Larsen's 1979 study continues to hold true, there is little agreement on actual titles to be taught in library schools.[5] One good teaching approach would be a comparison of sources of various subject disciplines, noting how a subject field is organized in order to impart an understanding of reference sources.

Identification of sources should be explained making use of catalogs, for with real facility in use of a catalog, reference sources can be identified. Sources can be identified through the use of secondary reference sources as well so that the librarian will have experience with this technique in library school.[6]

Reference techniques on the desk, including both interviewing and the development of search strategies, also need to be taught. The librarian needs to know what the best ways of answering specific types of questions are and why one solution is better than others.

The REFSIM project developed a teaching model in an online database that assists in teaching the identification of sources for specific types of questions.[7] It simulates the schemata in a reference librarian's brain through what have been called rules. Situations are set up so that if something is true, then certain possibilities should be tried and in certain order of priority. While many questions can be answered in this way, certain complex questions defy following a set of rules. However, the library school student needs to learn that there are alternative ways of assisting students to find information.

Reference librarians need to know how books are selected and acquired in a library and something about the management of book budgets—that is, a knowledge of sources of book information and evaluation, vendors, approval plans, etc. As part of their job they may select materials for the general or reference collection.

Library school education should inculcate the larger picture and theory of what constitutes library and information science rather than an endless number of titles and specifics that will soon be out of date or no longer pertinent.

Librarians need to learn about libraries as systems, including how they are managed. In fact, it is useful for them to learn some management skills. And every course should include an explanation of how the knowledge taught therein applies in a library.

The library student should learn about librarianship as a profession, the opportunities available and the organizations which support the profession. They should learn about professional ethics for librarianship.

Word processing can be an advantageous skill, although there have been reference librarians who did not even know how to type.

Professional education will not necessarily make anyone an operational librarian the first day on the job, but certain basic competencies are considered to be essential.[8] The hiring library will need to give the new librarian a certain amount of orientation and training. It is appropriate that such training be accomplished on the job rather than in library school.[9]

Even when a librarian's education has been completed and her initial training is finished, her learning must not end. At that point she may be an effective librarian, but if she does nothing to keep her skills and knowledge up to date, she will gradually become unqualified.[10] Librarians need to take continuing education courses and attend training sessions, workshops, and conferences to stay sharp and current. They need to read the professional literature of librarianship and of their subject fields. As professionals, reference librarians, perhaps in consultation with colleagues and supervisors, should develop a plan for their own continuing education and training as part of their total career plan.[11]

# Chapter 18.

# Obtaining a Position

After completing a professional degree, the next step in becoming a reference librarian is obtaining a position. This task is not particularly easy.

First, new graduates will prepare a résumé of education, experience and references. There are books to assist with résumé preparation, or faculty members may help. Then they will have to make decisions about the type of position they will seek: location, size of school, general or special. They will have to find out what is available. There will be postings at library schools, in the professional literature, on national and state hotlines, and on the World Wide Web.*

After matching their desires and qualifications to the listed jobs, they will apply to the positions listed that interest them, usually sending their résumé. In fact, even before taking their professional education, prospective librarians may have decided what type of position they are interested in and prepared for it. Special preparation may give them an edge in their applications for positions.

After the posted deadline, the hiring library will review the applications, which will probably be quite numerous. The personnel officer, peer committee, or head of the department will review the applications and choose several applicants on whom they would like to have more information. At this point, letters of reference will be requested.

A much shorter list of candidates will be prepared next, and the candidates most suited to the position will be asked to the campus for an interview. At an interview, the candidates will meet various librarians singly or in groups and will be asked about their training

*http://www.ala.org@ACRL.html. Select C&RL News and then Job Postings.

and experience. The candidates will also use the interview as an opportunity to find out as much as possible about the duties of the position, the management style in the library and department and the surrounding community. Candidates should also determine the status of librarians in the institution and whether there is a librarians' association or union. As an alternative to the campus visit interview, candidates may be interviewed for positions at national or state library association conventions, perhaps followed by a campus visit. The interviews allow the hiring libraries to learn about the candidates and vice versa.

The same groups who reviewed the applications or those that took part in the interviews make recommendations for hiring and a decision is made, usually by the library administration. From the candidate's perspective, the position either is offered or is not. If it is not, the candidate can treat the interview as a learning experience which will help him improve his performance at the next interview. If offered the position, the candidate can do some negotiation about salary and career steps, if there are such, but until candidates have had some experience, they will usually accept what is offered. Some institutions may pay moving costs.

The application ordeal is finally over and the position accepted with the date to begin work agreed upon. New librarians will probably arrive at the new location a few days early in order to find a place to live and become acclimated to the city and the campus before the first day of work.

New librarians will be given at a minimum a desk in a room of desks or a cubicle among other cubicles; at maximum they may be given a private office complete with a computer terminal and printer hooked up to a modem or directly into a network. They will be introduced to the staff, some of whom they will have met when interviewing for the position. Sometimes new librarians are given an organization chart and are told what positions other librarians hold or what responsibilities they have, but the organization chart says nothing about the employee power structure or the internal politics of the library.

The new librarian will receive a job description or assignment of duties indicating to whom she reports and whom she supervises.

Depending on the library, someone (the head of reference or a librarian designated to orient new personnel) will give the new librarian orientation and training extending over a week or several weeks.

# Chapter 19.
# Training and Responsibilities

## Training

Once new librarians are on board, they receive a certain amount of orientation and training. As suggested earlier, their professional education does not necessarily make them operational librarians on the first day of a job although they are expected to have certain basic competencies.[1] Certain kinds of training are more appropriately accomplished on the job than in library school.[2] If the reference head does not actually do the initial training, a mentor can be appointed to work with the new librarian. There is an extensive literature both on training the new librarian and on the provision of training programs for staff within the library.[3]

Suggestions for this training can be found in an article by Walters and Barnes.[4] In discussing the training program for interns at the University of California Los Angeles Medical Library program, the authors explain that goals for the training program were set up with behavioral objectives which define the performance desired. For each objective, competencies were identified. Structured guidelines were developed to achieve the competencies and criteria were set for evaluating their success.[5]

Britt, in a handbook developed for the University of California at Berkeley libraries, recommends having a written training plan such as the one she developed.[6] Her plan begins with orientation to the institution, the library, the department and unit supported by an orientation packet for new employees (suggestions for inclusion are listed). As in the UCLA program, objectives are recommended based on the employee's job description with a scheduled training program to achieve the objectives. Britt includes forms that can be used to develop training programs for specific jobs.

It is best, then, for reference departments to have a plan for training the new librarian so that the objectives are stated and the activities to achieve the objectives take place within a comfortable timetable, not just the first few days. In some cases sample questions are used as activities to acquaint new librarians with questions they will often be asked at the reference desk or to familiarize them with the library's whole range of reference materials. The policies, standards and procedures developed by the department assist the head in orienting the new librarian to the practices at the institution. They should all be part of the orientation packet which the new employee is given.

The training discussed to this point is primarily aimed at ensuring that the new librarian is effective on the desk or assisting patrons through a knowledge of techniques and resources. Other aspects of the new librarian's position which have been discussed will require a thorough introduction as well.

The goals and objectives for the program to which the librarian is assigned should be presented. The activities already in place should be described and the procedures for carrying out the activities detailed. As an example, for collection development librarians, the orientation packet should carefully delineate their responsibilities as to contacting the faculty and the level of knowledge they are expected to have of the instructional programs and the collections that support them. For instruction, courses and contacts or procedures for in-class instruction may be in place. The new librarians need to be sure they understand the responsibilities of their assignment.

They will also need to know the requirements for promotion or salary increases. To understand these requirements and responsibilities, they can benefit from having a mentor. Department heads are logical mentors because it is usually they who help librarians prepare for evaluation and who actually evaluate their performance.

While models can be used for this mentoring, it is up to the individual new librarian to determine how she meets her responsibilities and what contributions she will make after she understands what is expected of her. If librarians are enthusiastic about their work, their performance will be the result of their enthusiasm for the job rather than a calculated attempt for advancement.

## *Requirements for Advancement*

In most libraries, librarians are evaluated on the quality of their performance, professional service and scholarship.[7] Professional librarians will be required to perform their basic duties at a high level, but they also need to make contributions to the library, university and profession. Scholarship and resultant publications or presentations may be required.

It is the faculty status model which has shaped these wide responsibilities for the profession. Faculty status has been an issue in the library profession for a good many years and continues to be.[8] The Association of College and Research Libraries has developed standards for faculty status.[9] A large portion of universities and colleges throughout the country provide faculty or academic status.[10]

Through faculty status, librarians become partners with faculty in the education program of a campus. Faculty status provides librarians with tenure, support for pursuing research and professional activities, salaries on a par with other faculty members, and the ability to take part in the governance of the institution on the same level as other faculty members. For this parity with the faculty, schools often require their librarians to have advanced subject degrees in addition to their professional degrees.

Some universities have given librarians academic status rather than faculty status, presumably to recognize differences in preparation and tenure requirements, to avoid pay equity, or because they do not wish to accept librarians into full faculty status. These universities may provide tenure ranks and support for scholarship and professional participation so that in some measure librarians have some of the same benefits as faculty status.

## LIBRARY SERVICE

There are many different administrative or service committees to which a reference librarian may be assigned in a library. If there is a librarians' association (a quasi-academic senate), professional committees may overlap with administrative committees in the same area or be designated as administrative committees. Probably the more important of these committees are the Personnel, which is involved in the hiring or library review process for tenure, advancement or promotion, and the Professional Development and Travel, which makes recommendations for support of those activities. Reference librarians may take an active part in a librarians' association depending on their interest, perhaps to the extent of holding an office.

Librarians may be allowed to serve on some campuswide committees or attend faculty senate meetings even if they do not have faculty status.[11] Campuses differ in this regard. While the faculty may be willing for librarians to be members of some committees, they may decide a librarian has no business on "important" ones such as the Committee on Academic Personnel or the Committee on Educational Policy. The latter, ironically, would seem an ideal committee for librarian membership because of the effects its decisions have on the library.

Committee involvement may be mandatory or voluntary. And although it may be officially voluntary, in the institutions at which merit increases and promotions are based on participation in library-wide service, university service, and service beyond the local scene in the profession as well as on job performance, librarians know they must take part.

## PROFESSIONAL SERVICE

Reference librarians will be expected to take an active part in professional organizations on a local or national level.[12] They will not only attend professional meetings, but will present programs, serve on committees, or run for office. Every year the ACRL publishes a long list of committees which members can take part in. In participating in professional organizations, librarians contribute their skill and knowledge to the profession by sharing their experiences. Having developed a level of expertise in a facet of library service, librarians will be willing to plan workshops to share their knowledge.[13] Workshops may address such topics as library skills workbooks, one-shot lectures, slide tape shows, teaching difficult subjects, sources in a particular subject field, serving nontraditional patrons, use of CDs or networks, or any number of others.[14] While this service might appear to be obligatory, most reference librarians enjoy being on committees, attending conferences and sharing their expertise.

Since committee membership in a professional organization usually requires attendance at both the annual and midwinter meetings of such national organizations as the American Library Association, librarians need to consider support for these activities. Before leaping into attendance and participation, reference librarians must determine how much their institution is willing to provide funds for these activities. Time off with pay is usual, but beyond that libraries' policies vary. If a library administration has assigned a librarian to attend, it may consider the trip a library assignment and pay travel expenses, the cost of the conference, and a per diem. If the library administration believes in this type of participation, it will make some funds available, trying to make a fair distribution among the librarians. Each institution is different. Obviously if librarians are giving a paper or chairing a meeting or committee, they are more likely to receive support from their institutions.

Having determined the level of support in their libraries, librarians will then have to decide how much of their own time and funds they are willing to commit. It is perhaps ironic that the librarians with the highest salaries are more likely to have funds available to them.

## SCHOLARSHIP AND RESEARCH

Librarians are also expected to perform research or publish. The results of scholarship by librarians may include books, chapters of books, journal articles, annotated bibliographies, translations, book reviews, literature guides, papers presented, workshops conducted, poster sessions, and other accomplishments. Much of the scholarship of librarians concerns activities of a practical nature, often proposing changes, reporting how changes have been made, or sharing program ideas with members of the profession.[15] The scholarship requirement may be daunting for the new librarian, but their enthusiasm for their work will naturally lead them to take part in many of these activities.

The degree to which the library supports research and publishing will also have to be determined. Can librarians take time during the work day to do research and write an article? Can they use the services of a typist? Can they use copy machine, telephone, and fax machine?

## *Professional Development*

In a paper some years ago, this author suggested that like Alice and the red queen, librarians were being forced to run faster and faster just to stay in the same place.[16] Now, no matter how fast librarians run, they cannot stay in the same place because it no longer exists. In the rapidly changing environment in which they work, reference librarians must constantly learn new skills and deepen their knowledge. Rothstein suggests that today's librarians must know a great deal more than previously.[17] In the process, they are redesigning and changing reference librarianship.

Librarians can elect to take courses at their institutions and can be encouraged to do so by being given time off to attend the classes or by being given scholarships for tuition.[18] If a library school is nearby, specialized work in library and information science may be supported. Conferences and workshops off campus can also be useful for learning. These can be offered by professional associations, state agencies, library schools or commercial groups. Workshops have been part of regional meetings, state library conventions, and the national American Library Association conferences. Of course, all of these conferences have a great deal more to offer than merely workshops. Any librarian attending a conference will experience the excitement of taking part in the exchange of ideas in the profession. They will hear the professional leaders speak and will meet colleagues from far and wide who may be facing the same problems as they are.

The profession has changed rapidly in the past twenty years. In two areas in particular, bibliographic instruction and online searching, reference librarians have had to learn from scratch, sometimes even if they are recent graduates. Now they must learn to travel the superhighways of Internet. Particularly in the area of instruction, until library schools provide adequate coursework in instruction as the profession recommends, librarians need to become proficient in instruction on their own.[19]

Workshops were extremely helpful in the early stages of the bibliographic instruction movement and continue to be when a new librarian must learn from an experienced librarian.[20] From the early book edited by John Lubans to the present day, a vast literature has developed addressing the whole field of bibliographic instruction.[21] Reference librarians can learn from this extensive literature as well as from using books and articles as models in the development of programs. Workshops have been sponsored by local library instruction clearinghouses, and LOEX sponsors an annual conference and publishes the papers.

Librarians have quickly had to become knowledgeable about computers, hypertext, software and criteria for purchasing CD-ROMs. Searching databases has introduced a heavy burden as librarians have had to learn the protocols and special command language of specific databases. For example, a University of California reference librarian might have to know the unique protocols for OCLC, RLIN, MELVYL (including its many databases variant protocols), the local online catalog, Orion, Gladis, DIALOG, BRS, SDC, WILSON-LINE, Silverplatter, and others.

It is no wonder that in purchasing databases on CD-ROM librarians often choose products using the same software (Silverplatter, for example, or WILSONLINE). Actually CD-ROM producers have simplified searching procedures and provided online instruction to assist patrons in the use of their database. But even if a database is easily accessed, patrons are not always successful in performing searches. Sometimes producers have offered trial use of a database to persuade librarians to purchase them.

In order to keep current, librarians need to understand networks and networking, Internet, Bitnet or any local networks which have special databases mounted on them. Handbooks and workshops have been prepared to teach Internet use.[22] Local networks provide remote access on a campus to central databases where information of local interest can be mounted.[23] National and international networks, besides providing access to databases, provide for the exchange of ideas and selective dissemination of information to electronic mailboxes.

Until the late 1970s and early 1980s, few librarians had formal training in the use of online databases. Library administrations have attempted to solve this learning problem in a variety of ways: sending librarians to training sessions sponsored by vendors or by the profession, bringing in experts to teach, or using their most highly trained staff members to teach others in the library who need to know. Individual librarians can add to their training by reading manuals and articles and by practicing. The decline in online searching that has accompanied the growth of CD-ROM use has made it more difficult for experienced searchers to maintain their skills and exceedingly difficult for new librarians to acquire sophisticated searching skills. Libraries now are also less willing to spend substantial sums on vendor workshops. Internet workshops are more likely to receive support at the present time.

Practicing can also be costly for the library if the database used has to be paid for (though from time to time, vendors provide practice time at cheaper prices). However, practice is necessary if librarians are to become proficient and effective searchers. Parceling out the responsibility for database searching can be another solution; a library can assign specific librarians to be experts in the protocols of a given system or database.

The problem with learning protocols for the librarian is not just to keep the facility to search a seldom used database, but to keep current on new innovations and improvements. Learning to use new systems is an ongoing self-education task. The speed of change is currently so great that between the writing of this book and its publication, a number of new developments of importance to librarians will surely have occurred.

Attendance at in-house training sessions is of great value in keeping librarians up to date in the area of both knowledge and skills. These sessions may be held several times when a topic as large as online searching is being taught, or may simply be incorporated into monthly update workshops. The latter may also introduce new reference tools such as a database on CD-ROM or a new wrinkle on the online catalog. These sessions may further provide refreshers on older tools such as a microform collection and its access (the HRAF file, for example). They can provide an opportunity for one department to introduce itself to another. This latter type of presentation is a real help in encouraging the referral of difficult reference questions.

While associations sponsor programs, individual librarians within the organization will determine needs and plan programs to meet them. The Association of College and Research Libraries has presented continuing education programs both as preconferences to the annual convention and as workshops during the convention. The California Clearinghouse for Bibliographic Instruction not only collects materials, but presents workshops throughout the state, and LOEX has an annual meeting on library instruction. Online vendors and database producers have a full schedule of training programs throughout the United States and abroad.

Reading the professional literature is important for professional development. In some initial training programs, articles are selected to be read by the participants.[24] Librarians are not expected to spend every evening reading *RQ*, but unless the institution allows time for it, some professional reading may have to be done after library hours. In some libraries, the only acceptable reading for slow hours at the desk is professional literature, but with recent budget crunches there may be no slow hours.

Librarians who are interested in professional literature will read; others may have to be encouraged by providing scheduled time for reading, circulating issues of the journals or perhaps setting up a work station with the latest journal issues available.[25]

# Notes

## Preface

1. Alfred Willis and Eugene E. Matysek, Jr. "Place and Functionality of Reference Services," in Anne Grodzins Lipow, ed. *Rethinking Reference in Academic Libraries* (Berkeley, Ca.: Library Solutions Press, 1993), 185-89.

2. Charles A. Bunge, "A Reply to Willis and Matysek," in Lipow, pp. 191-93.

## Introduction to Part I

1. Charles Anderson, "The Exchange: Stupid Questions," *RQ* 25 (Summer 1986): 433.

2. All profession positions take time to learn to be proficient. For doctors, their internship is usually two years, and their residencies are three years. In business, salary scales and requirements for replacement can be based on the length of time it takes to learn the job.

3. Barbara M. Robinson, "Reference Services: A Model of Question Handling," *RQ* 29 (Fall 1989): 48–61; Gerald Jahoda, "Rules for Performing Steps in the Reference Process," *Reference Librarian* 25/26 (1989): 557–67; James Benson and Ruth Maloney, "Principles of Searching," *RQ* 14 (Summer 1975): 316–320; Gerald Jahoda and Judith Schick Braunagel, *The Librarian and Reference Queries* (New York: Academic Press, 1980).

## Chapter 1

1. The word "student" will primarily be used in the text rather than "patron," "user" or "client" because students are the main clientele requesting assistance in an academic library.

2. Virginia Boucher, "Nonverbal Communication and the Library Reference Interview," *RQ* 16 (Fall 1976): 27–32; Joanna Lopez Munoz, "The

Significance of Nonverbal Communication in the Reference Interview," *RQ* 16 (Spring 1977): 220–24; Helen M. Gothberg, "Immediacy: A Study of Communication Effect on the Reference Process," *Journal of Academic Librarianship* 2 (July 1976): 126–29; Stuart Glogoff, "Communication Theory's Role in the Reference Interview," *Drexel Library Quarterly* 19 (Spring 1983): 56–72.

3. Elaine Z. Jennerich, "Before the Answer: Evaluating the Reference Process," *RQ* 19 (Summer 1980): 360–66.

4. Robert Chadbourne, "The Problem Patron: How Much Problem, How Much Patron," *Wilson Library Bulletin* 64 (June 1990): 59–60. Joseph J. Mika and Bruce A. Shuman, "Legal Issues Affecting Libraries and Librarians: Employment Law, Liability & Insurance, Contracts, and Problem Patrons," *American Libraries* 19 (April 1988): 314–17.

5. During the late sixties, libraries were plagued by endless bomb threats, and even in the nineties bomb threats are still received.

6. Mary Jo Lynch, "Reference Interviews in Public Libraries," *Library Quarterly* 48 (April 1978): 128. Howell determined in her study (Benita J. Howell, Edward B. Reeves, and John Van Willigen, "Fleeting Encounters: A Role Analysis of Reference Librarian–Patron Interaction," *RQ* 16 (Winter 1976: 126) that only one third of the questions needed negotiation. St. Clair gives the figure of 40 percent requiring a professional librarian in Jeffrey W. St. Clair and Rao Aluri, "Staffing the Reference Desk: Professionals or Nonprofessionals?," *Journal of Academic Librarianship* 3 (July 1977): 151.

7. Lynch, "Reference Interviews," pp. 120, 140; Robert S. Taylor, "Question-Negotiation and Information Seeking in Libraries," *College & Research Libraries* 19 (May 1968): 183.

8. CD-ROM means compact disc read-only memory. The compact discs are read into a computer so that they may be searched by means of commands (protocols) provided for searching. CD-ROM can also be mounted on local area networks (LANs) for use by students at several stations.

9. Undergraduate students may not realize when pursuing subjects involving Russia or Mexico that they will find some materials in Russian and Spanish.

10. Jahoda, *Reference Queries*, p. 117; Fred Oser, "Referens Simplex or the Mysteries of Reference Interviewing Revealed," *Reference Librarian* 16 (Winter 1986): 65; William A. Katz, *Introduction to Reference Work*, vol. II, 4th ed. (New York: McGraw-Hill, 1982), p. 47; Robinson, "Reference Services," p. 51.

11. Taylor, "Question-Negotiation," p. 185; Geraldine B. King, "Open & Closed Questions: The Reference Interview," *RQ* 12 (Winter 1972): 158.

12. Thomas Lee Eichman, "The Complex Nature of Opening Reference Questions," *RQ* 17 (Spring 1978): 218.

13. Marilyn Domas White, "The Reference Encounter Model," *Drexel Library Quarterly* 19 (Spring 1983): 38–55.

14. George S. Hawley, *The Referral Process in Libraries: A Characterization and Exploration of Related Facts* (Chicago: American Library Association, 1983), p. 41.

15. Lydia Olszak, "Mistakes and Failures at the Reference Desk," *RQ* 31 (Fall 1991): 43–44.

16. Marilyn Domas White, "The Dimensions of the Reference Interview," *RQ* 20 (Summer 1981): 377.

17. White, "Dimensions," p. 380.

18. In her study, Lynch found that 90 percent of the questions were closed questions. Lynch, "Reference Interviews," p. 135.

19. Brenda Dervin and Patricia Dewdney, "Neutral Questioning: A New Approach to the Reference Interview," *RQ* 25 (Summer 1986): 508.

20. Bryce Allen, "Text Structures and the User-Intermediary Interaction," *RQ* 27 (Summer 1988): 540.

21. Allen, "Text Structure," p. 538.

22. Eichman, "The Complex Nature," p. 219; Theodore P. Peck, "Counseling Skills Applied to Reference," *RQ* 14 (Spring 1975): 234.

# Chapter 2

1. Richard E. Bopp and Linda Smith, eds., *Reference and Information Services: An Introduction* (Englewood, Colo.: Libraries Unlimited, 1991), p. 75.

2. A lengthy group of questions have been presented with reference titles in Thomas P. Slavens, ed., *Reference Interviews, Questions, and Materials*, 2nd ed. (Metuchen, N.J.: Scarecrow Press, 1985).

3. Richard L. Derr, "Questions: Definitions, Structure, and Classification," *RQ* 24 (Winter 1984): 186–90.

4. Anne B. Piternick, "Decision Factors Favoring the Use of Online Sources for Providing Information," *RQ* 29 (Summer 1990): 534–544.

5. White, "Reference Encounter Model," pp. 38–55.

6. Ibid., p. 51.

7. Because reference work may be considered the core task for the profession as a whole, the "public face" of the occupation, reference librarians must recognize that their performance on a desk can enhance the status of librarians in their own library as well as in the whole profession of librarianship. Brian Nielsen, "Teacher or Intermediary: Alternative Professional Models in the Information Age," *College & Research Libraries* 43 (May 1982): 184–85.

8. In an online catalog, bibliographic information is stored electronically by what are called fields (sections of the record) identified by tags so they can be located for searching. The fields include author, title and subject fields among other fields such as LC number or call number.

9. Usha Gupta and Lutishoor Salisbury, "Is FirstSearch Really Attractive?" *College & Research Libraries News* 53 (July/August 1992): 461–464.

10. MELVYL (UC online union catalog) provides WorldCat making use of its own command language.

11. Mary Page, "A Personal View of the Internet," *College & Research Libraries News* 54 (March 1993): 127–32.

12. Roy Tennant, John Ober, and Anne G. Lipow, *Crossing the Internet Threshold: an Instructional Handbook* (Berkeley, Ca.: Library Solutions Press, 1993); Brendan P. Kehoe, *Zen and the Art of the Internet: A Beginner's Guide*,

2nd ed. (Englewood Cliffs, N.J.: PTR Prentice Hall, 1993); "A Hands-On Introduction to the Internet," Workshop, Fall 1993, California State University, Fullerton.

13. Julie Still and Jan Alexander, "Integrating Internet into Reference: Policy Issues," *College & Research Libraries News* 54 (March 1993): 139–40.

14. Paul Fehrmann, "Internet Resources for Psychology," *College & Research Libraries News* 54 (October 1993): 510–11. "Internet Resources for Architecture Studies," *College & Research Libraries News* 54 (April 1993): 189.

15. Archie G. Rugh, "Reference Standards & Reference Work," *Library Journal* 101 (July 1976): 1498.

16. The G.K. Hall Company was a leader in the publication of library subject catalogs.

17. In preparing this book, the author used a number of book bibliographies and bibliographies in books and periodicals.

18. William A. Katz, *Introduction to Reference Work*, vol. I: "Basic Information Sources," 4th ed. (New York: McGraw-Hill, 1982), p. 47.

19. Combining terms making use of "and" limits the search; use of "or" broadens the search. Sometimes the "and" is merely inferred when more than one term is used.

20. "Guidelines for a Database Search Guide," *RQ* 26 (Summer 1987): 441–43.

21. One library's ready reference searching is discussed in Sara Brownmiller, A. Craig Hawbaker and others, "Online-Ready-Reference Searching in an Academic Library," *RQ* 24 (Spring 1985): 320–26.

22. G. Margaret Porter, "What Does Electronic Access to Bibliographic Information Cost?," *College & Research Libraries News* 52 (February 1991): 90–92.

23. Thomas G. Kirk, "College Libraries and the New Technology," *College & Research Libraries News* 55 (April 1994): 196–97.

## Chapter 3

1. Stuart A. Stiffler, "A Book Is a Book Is a Reference Book," *RQ* 11 (Summer 1972): 341–43.

2. Examples: Books on résumé preparation or the city directory.

3. Marcia J. Bates, "What Is a Reference Book? A Theoretical and Empirical Analysis," *RQ* 26 (Fall 1986): 54.

4. Rolland E. Stevens and Linda C. Smith, *Reference Work in the University Library* (Littleton, Colo.: Libraries Unlimited, 1986); James M. Doyle and George H. Grimes, *Reference Resources: A Systematic Approach* (Metuchen, N.J.: Scarecrow Press, 1976); William A. Katz, *Introduction to Reference Work*, vol. I: "Basic Information Sources," 6th ed. (New York: McGraw-Hill, 1992).

5. Richard L. Hopkins, "Ranking the Reference Books: Methodologies for Identifying 'Key' Reference Sources," *Reference Librarian* 33 (1991): 77–102;

John C. Larsen, "Information Sources Currently Studied in General Reference Courses," *RQ* 18 (Summer 1979): 341–48.

6. Substantiated in Archie G. Rugh, "Catalog, Bibliography, or Index," *RQ* 13 (Fall 1973): 27–30.

7. The following subject headings are used for the *Social Sciences Index*: Social sciences—Indexes, Periodicals—Indexes, Social sciences—Periodicals—Index. These headings would not help you find material in ethnology or sociology without generalizing these specific subjects.

8. Zheng Fan with Nancy Slater, "Reference Queries, Experience, and Secondary Reference Books," *Reference Librarian* 22 (1988): 271–82.

9. Eugene P. Sheehy, *Guide to Reference Books*, 10th ed. (Chicago: American Library Association, 1986), Robert Balay, ed., *Guide to Reference Books: Covering Materials from 1985–1990* (Chicago: American Library Association, 1992); and Albert John Walford, *Guide to Reference Material*, 5th ed.(London: Library Association, 1989).

10. *New York Public Library Desk Reference* (New York: Webster's New World, 1989).

11. Theodore Besterman, *World Bibliography of Bibliographies* ..., 4th ed. (Lausanne: Societas bibliographica, 1965–66).

12. *Directories in Print, 14th ed.* (Detroit: Gale Research, 1997).

13. *Biography and Genealogy Master Index, 2nd ed.* (Detroit: Gale Research, 1980).

14. *Gale Directory of Databases* (Detroit: Gale Research, 1993).

15. Some instructors of research classes bypass this problem of identifying indexes by simply recommending titles for various topics and instructing the students on how to use the indexes.

16. The records in this database now include the information in the long display about where a periodical is indexed.

17. The HRAF is an information file for anthropology on world cultures, which are identified by alphanumeric codes. Cultural traits are identified by numeric codes for retrieval of information from source documents. Some of the file is now available on CD-ROM.

## Chapter 4

1. Compare definitions in George S. Hawley, *The Referral Process in Libraries: A Characterization and Exploration of Related Factors* (Chicago: American Library Association, 1983), p. 28, and Thomas Childers, *Information & Referral: Public Libraries* (Norwood, N.J.: Ablex, 1983), p. 1.

2. American Library Association, Reference and Adult Service Division, Standards Committee, "A Commitment to Information Service: Developmental Guidelines," *RQ* 18 (Spring 1979): 276.

3. "Standards and Guidelines Subcommittee Releases Draft of New Document," *RASD Update* 12 (Apr./June 1991): 27.

4. Charles R. McClure and Peter Hernon, *Improving the Quality of Reference Service for Government Publications* (Chicago: American Library Association, 1983), 151–153.

5. Peter Hernon and Charles R. McClure, "Referral Services in U.S. Academic Depository Libraries: Findings, Implications, and Research Needs," *RQ* 22 (Winter 1982): 161–162.

6. M. J. Dustin, "Cooperative Reference Services Committee," *RQ* 24 (Spring 1985): 279–82.

7. When a patron wanted a book review citation from the index to foreign book reviews in storage, someone at the storage facility should have been able to search for the citation.

8. Jan Kemp and Dennis Dillon, "Collaboration and the Accuracy Imperative: Improving Reference Service Now," *RQ* 29 (Fall 1989): 69.

9. There are, of course, catalogs of manuscript collections or bibliographies of special materials such as trade catalogs which libraries have in their reference collections which can be useful.

10. *Directory of Information and Referral Services in the United States and Canada* (Phoenix: Alliance of Information and Referral Services, 1989–90); Lee Ash, ed., *Subject Collections*, 7th ed. rev. and enl. (New Providence, N.J.: R.R. Bowker, 1993), 2 vols.; *Encyclopedia of Associations* 31 (Detroit: Gale Research, 1996).

11. Kathleen Dunn and Myra White, "Experimenting with Reference Referral in a Multitype Environment," *College and Research Library News* 52 (June 1991): 363–65.

12. The Reference and Government Publication departments at UCSB routinely exchanged personnel before the two departments were combined.

13. Dunn and White, pp. 363–365.

14. A UCSB example prior to the Government Publications Department combining with Reference.

15. Hawley, *Referral Process*, pp. 94–96, 99–100.

16. Once, the author called Document Delivery Service at UC Berkeley about a quote. The staff found the volume and read the quote, saving the patron time and effort. The patron was a faculty member, which brings up the whole question of service to client groups.

17. Teresa L. Demo and Charles R. McClure, "Information and Referral in the Academic Library: Lessons in Attitude and Service from the Public Library," *Reference Librarian* 21 (1988): 103.

18. Ralph Gers and Lillie J. Seward, "Improving Reference Performance: Results of a Statewide Study," *Library Journal* 110 (Nov. 1, 1989): 32–35.

19. Patricia Gebhard, Art Anthony, and Gary Peete, "Networking in the Microcosm: Reference Referrals," *RQ* 17 (Spring 1978): 197–201.

20. Dunn and White, pp. 363–365.

## *Chapter 5*

1. Ralph Gers and Lillie J. Seward, "Improving Reference Performance: Results of a Statewide Study," *Library Journal* 110 (Nov. 1, 1985): 35.

2. Levels of service from the 1930s to the present day are discussed in James Rettig, "A Theoretical Model and Definition of the Reference Process," *RQ* 18 (Fall 1978): 19–29.

3. Mary Jo Lynch, "Toward a Definition of Service; Academic Library Reference Policy Statements," *RQ* 11 (Spring 1972): 222–26.

4. The discouragement of pointing is mentioned in Dave Strickler, "What I Learned Working in a Bookstore," *Library Journal* 117 (June 15, 1992): 48.

5. Diana M. Thomas, Ann T. Hinckley and Elizabeth R. Eisenback, *The Effective Reference Librarian* (New York: Academic Press, 1981), p. 1.

6. Robert S. Taylor, "Question-Negotiation and Information Seeking in Libraries," *College & Research Libraries* 29 (May 1968): 188; Rebecca R. Martin, "The Paradox of Public Service: Where Do We Draw the Line?" *College & Research Libraries* 51 (Jan. 1990): 25.

7. Jo Bell Whitlatch, *The Role of the Academic Reference Librarian.* (Westport, Conn.: Greenwood Press, 1990), p. 64.

8. The author has never personally favored handing a patron a source and saying get on with it. Of course, librarians can say to look in *Contemporary Authors* and give the students the call number or show where it is on the shelf, but how much better service to show the patron the cumulative indexes and where the sets cited are located.

9. F. W. Lancaster and others, "Searching Databases on CD-ROM: Comparison of the Results of End-User Searching with Results from Two Modes of Searching by Skilled Intermediaries," *RQ* 33 (Spring 1994): 383.

10. Ibid., p. 382.

11. Benita J. Howell and others, "Fleeting Encounters—A Role Analysis of Reference Librarian–Patron Interaction," *RQ* 16 (Winter 1976): 127–28.

12. Ibid., p. 127.

13. Barbara Robinson, "Reference Services: A Model of Question Handling," *RQ* 29 (Fall 1989): 51.

## Chapter 6

1. Christopher W. Nolan, "Closing the Reference Interview: Implications for Policy and Practice," *RQ* 31 (Summer 1992): 513–23.

2. For example, online searching for patrons who are not part of the library's basic clientele.

## Chapter 7

1. Anne Grodzin Lipow, "Prestige, Appointments, and Ready Professional Attention," *Journal of Academic Librarianship* 11 (May 1985): 70–71; Joseph Rosenblum, "Stay Close to Your Desk and Never Go to Sea," *Journal of Academic Librarianship* 11 (May 1985): 72–73; Mary Biggs, "Replacing the Fast Fact Drop-in with Gourmet Information Service: A Symposium," *Journal of Academic Librarianship* 11 (May 1985): 68–71; Barbara J. Ford, "Reference Beyond (and Without) the Reference Desk," *College & Research Libraries* 47

(Sept. 1986): 491–94; William Miller, "What's Wrong with Reference: Coping with Success and Failure at the Reference Desk," *American Libraries* 15 (May 1984): 306.

2. Not only is this the average time, but when librarians have been observed on a busy desk, they appear to have a built-in alarm system which keeps them to brief encounters.

3. Bill Bailey, "Thesis Practicum and the Librarian's Role," *Journal of Academic Librarianship* 11 (May 1985): 79–81; Kathleen Bergen and Barbara MacAdam, "One-on-One Term Paper Assistance Programs," *RQ* 24 (Spring 1985): 333–39.

4. Adeane Bregman and Barbara Mento, "Reference Roving at Boston College," *College & Research Libraries News* 53 (November 1992): 634–35, 637; Jennii Ramirez "Reference Rover: The Hesitant Patron's Best Friend," *College & Research Libraries News* 55 (June 1994): 354–57.

# Chapter 8

1. Expert systems are simulated reference encounters on computers. Users type in their requests or select from a menu of possibilities. The system is programmed to give answers.

2. William L. Whitson, "Alternative Models of Reference Service: A Proposal," unpublished paper posted on Internet (Berkeley, Ca., February 22, 1994). Available from COLLIBL@WILLAMETTE.edu.

3. UCLA set up its catalog assistant desk when its recent materials were published in a microfiche catalog. UCSB has a desk for assistance with the local online catalog, MELVYL and the terminals for using CD-ROMs.

4. The discussion of providing an information desk at Brandeis University mentions this factor in Virginia Massey-Burzio, "Reference Encounters of a Different Kind: A Symposium," *Journal of Academic Librarianship* 18 (November 1992): 276–86.

5. Compare Oberg's definition (note 32) in Larry Oberg, "The Emergence of the Paraprofessional in Academic Libraries: Perceptions and Realities," *College & Research Libraries* 53 (March 1992): 111.

6. Oberg, "The Emergence," pp. 99–112; Larry R. Oberg and others, "The Role, Status, and Working Conditions of Paraprofessionals: A National Survey of Academic Libraries," *College & Research Libraries* 53 (May 1992): 215–38.

7. E. A. Halldorsson and M.E. Murfin, "The Performance of Professionals and Non-Professionals in the Reference Interview," *College & Research Libraries* 38 (Sept. 1977): 385–395. See also discussion in section on referrals.

8. William F. Heinlein, "Using Students in Academic Reference," *RQ* 15 (Summer 1976): 325; Kathleen Coleman and Elizabeth Margutti, "Training Nonprofessionals for Reference Service," *RQ* 16 (Spring 1977): 217–19.

9. Allen B. Veaner, "Paradigm Lost, Paradigm Regained: A Persistent Personnel Issue in Academic Librarianship, II," *College & Research Libraries* 55 (September 1994): 389–402.

10. Dana E. Smith, "Reference Expert Systems: Humanizing Depersonalized Service," *Reference Librarian* 23 (1989): 190.

11. John Richardson, Jr., "Toward an Expert System for Reference Service: A Research Agenda for the 1990s," *College & Research Libraries* 50 (March 1989): 232.

12. Linda Brew MacDonald and others, *Teaching Technologies in Libraries: a Practical Guide* (Boston: G.K. Hall, 1991). Pages 206–09 discuss various available shells.

13. Dana E. Smith, "Reference Expert Systems," p. 188; Karen F. Smith, "Robot at the Reference Desk?," *College & Research Libraries* 47 (Sept. 1986): 487.

14. James R. Parrott, "REFSIM: A Bimodal Knowledge-based Reference Training and Consultation System," *RSR Reference Service Review* 16 (1988): 61–68.

15. Some databases on MELVYL are accessed by abbreviations (CC or MAGS), some by the term "use" (Use ERIC), others by use of the experimental mode (WORLDCAT).

16. Frank R. Allen and Rita H. Smith, "A Survey of Telephone Inquiries: Case Study and Operational Impact in an Academic Library Reference Department," *RQ* 32 (Spring 1993): 382–91.

17. Christine M. Roysdon and Laura Lee Elliott, "Electronic Integration of Library Services through a Campuswide Network," *RQ* 28 (Fall 1988): 82–93; Ann Bristow, "Academic Reference Service Over Electronic Mail," *College & Research Libraries News* 53 (November 1992): 631–32, 637.

18. Paul Frisch and John J. Small, "Voice Mail at the Reference Desk," *College & Research Libraries News* 55 ( June 1994): 343–45.

## *Chapter 9*

1. Richard L. Hopkins, "Ranking the Reference Books: Methodologies for Identifying 'Key' Reference Sources," *Reference Librarian* 33 (1991): 77–102.

2. Evan I. Farber, "A Keyword Index to the Reference Collection," *American Libraries* 18 ( June 1987): 440–41.

3. If keyword facility is already available on the local online catalog, a keyword index of reference materials is not necessary.

4. *Contemporary Literary Criticism* (Detroit: Gale Research, vols. 1–92, 1973–96).

5. *Twentieth-Century Literary Criticism* (Detroit: Gale Research, vols. 1–63, 1978–96).

6. *Dictionary of Literary Biography* (Detroit: Gale Research, vols. 1–167, 1978–96).

## Chapter 10

1. Individual librarians may have notebooks with information in them as reminders of questions or call numbers, but it would be much more useful if the whole department had access to this kind of information.

2. UCSB has a news screen from which can be found a list of style manuals, call numbers of dictionaries, hours, etc. MELVYL has a weather screen.

3. Examples at UCSB are early English books or Draper Manuscripts. UCLA, however, puts the reel number for early English book in their record available on MELVYL. Donald Wing, *Short-Title Catalog of Books Printed in England, Scotland, Ireland, Wales, and British America and of English Books Printed in Other Countries, 1641-1700* (New York: Columbia University Press, 1948). State Historical Society of Wisconsin Library, *The Preston and Virginia Papers of the Draper Collection of Manuscripts* (Madison: State Historical Society, 1915).

4. Joseph Sabin, *Biblioteca Americana, a Dictionary of Books Relating to America from Its Discovery to the Present Time* (New York, 1868–1936).

5. Patrons can be referred to the circulation department, but why refer the patron if the information is available in a leaflet in the manual?

6. Diana M. Thomas, Ann T. Hinckley, and Elizabeth R. Eisenbach, *The Effective Reference Librarian* (New York: Academic Press, 1981), p. 20.

7. Mark Stover and Esther Grassian, "Towards an Automated Reference Information System: Inmagic and the UCLA Ready-Reference Information Files," *RQ* 28 (Summer 1989): 517–27.

8. Evan I. Farber, "A Keyword Index to the Reference Collection," *American Libraries* 18 (June 1987): 440–41.

9. William R. Kinyon, Katharine E. Clark, Rosemary Loomis, and Susan J. Martin, "Producing In-House Indexes at Texas A&M," *RQ* 30 (Fall 1990): 51–59; A. Anneli Ahtola, "In-house Databases: An Opportunity for Progressive Libraries," *RQ* 29 (Fall 1989): 36–47.

10. Bill Katz and Anne Clifford, *Reference and Online Services Handbook: Guidelines, Policies and Procedures for Libraries, vol. 1* (New York: Neal-Schuman, 1982), p. xxvi.

11. Dave Strickler, "What I Learned Working in a Bookstore," *Library Journal* 117 (15 June 1992): 48.

12. Nolan's questions which he feels are necessary to be answered by policy statements are: 1. Is the reference department's mission to educate users or provide them answers? 2. Does the department provide different levels of service for different classes of users? 3. What is the minimum level of service that is professionally and institutionally appropriate? 4. How much time should reference librarians devote to handling individual questions? 5. What types of questions are considered out of bounds and not to be answered? 6. Is collaboration with or referral to other reference colleagues encouraged, or is the librarian on duty at the desk expected to handle any and all queries? 7. How much empathy for the user is expected of the librarian? Christopher W. Nolan, "Closing the Reference Interview: Implications for Policy and Practice," *RQ* 31 (Summer 1992): 519.

13. UCSB does not purchase books for recreational reading. UCB charges industrial borrowers a bibliographical service charge in addition to copy costs.

14. Mary Jo Lynch, "Toward a Definition of Service; Academic Library Reference Policy Statements," *RQ* 11 (Spring 1972): 222–26.

15. In *College & Research Libraries News* 53 (December 1992): 709–18.

16. Katz, *Reference and Online Services Handbook.*

17. A recent article discusses the development of standards at the University of Nebraska at Omaha. Carole A. Larson and Laura K. Dickson, "Developing Behavioral Reference Desk Performance Standards," *RQ* 33 (Spring 1994): 349–57. University of California Santa Barbara, "Reference Service Expectation," Feb. 5, 1990, unpublished; George Washington University, "Reference Service Performance Standards," unpublished; Case Western Reserve University, "Standards and Guidelines for Reference Services," unpublished, March 1988; University of Arizona Library, "CRD Reference Desk Performance Standards/Peer Review Form," unpublished, July 1982; University of California, Berkeley, "Public Service Policy Manual: Guidelines for Evaluating Reference Performance," unpublished, March 1990. Some of these standards are found in *Performance Evaluation in Reference Services in ARL Libraries: SPEC Kit 139* (Washington, D.C.: Association of Research Libraries Office of Management Studies, 1987).

18. University of Michigan, Alfred Taubman Medical Library, "Reference Standards," unpublished, included in ARL Spec Kit 139.

19. Carole A. Larson and Laura K. Dickson in *RQ* 33 (Spring 1994): 349–57.

20. Diane G. Schwartz and Dottie Eakin, "Reference Service Standards, Performance Criteria, and Evaluation," *Journal of Academic Librarianship* 12 (March 1986): 4–8.

21. American Library Association, Reference and Adult Services Division, Standards Committee, "A Commitment to Information Services: Developmental Guidelines," *RQ* 15 (Summer 1976): 327–30; *RQ* 18 (Spring 1979): 275–77.

22. Robert Klassen, "Standards for Reference Services," *Library Trends* 31 (Winter 1983): 421–28.

23. As an example, Archie G. Rugh, "Reference Standards & Reference Work," *Library Journal* 101 (July 1976): 1497–1500.

24. "Information Services for Information Consumers: Guidelines for Providers," *RQ* 30 (Winter 1990): 262–65.

25. James Rettig, "Behavioral Guidelines for Reference Librarians," *RQ* 32 (Fall 1992): 6.

26. Ibid.

27. Elizabeth Futas, "Ethics and Reference: No Easy Answers," *RQ* 29 (Fall 1989): 8.

28. Jonathan A. Lindsey and Ann E. Prentice, *Professional Ethics and Librarians* (Phoenix: Oryx, 1985) *The Reference Librarian* no. 4 was devoted to ethics. A bibliography was provided by Marie Garrett, "Applied and Professional Ethics: Resources for Research," *RQ* 29 (Summer 1990).

29. Futas, p. 8.

30. Quoted in "Ethics and Reference: No Easy Answers," *RQ* 29 (Fall 1989): 8–9. Also in American Library Association, *Handbook of Organization* (Chicago, American Library Association, 1990–91): 260.

31. Gillian S. Gremmels, "Reference in the Public Interest: An Examination of Ethics," *RQ* 30 (Spring 1991): 362–69.

32. Gayle J. Hardy and Judith Schiek Robinson, "Reference Services to Students: A Crucible for Ethical Inquiry," *RQ* 30 (Fall 1990): 82–87.

33. Futas, p. 10.

34. "Standards for Ethical Conduct for Rare Book, Manuscript, and Special Collections Libraries and Librarians," *College & Research Libraries News* 52 (December 1991): 721–29.

## Introduction to Part III

1. Brian Nielsen, "Teacher or Intermediary: Alternative Professional Models in the Information Age," *College & Research Libraries* 43 (May 1982): 183–91.

2. While the discussion of off-desk duties is based on the author's own experience, it was compared with activities discussed in Anthony W. Ferguson and John R. Taylor, "What Are You Doing? An Analysis of Activities of Public Service Librarians at a Medium-Sized Research Library," *Journal of Academic Librarianship* 6 (Mar. 1980): 24–29; Nancy Emmerick and Luella Davis, "A Survey of Academic Library Reference Service Practices. Preliminary Results," *RQ* 24 (Fall 1984): 74–75; Jeanie M. Welch, "Are All Reference Jobs Created Equal? A Comparison of Public and Academic Libraries," *RQ* 17 (Spring 1988): 397; and Paula Watson, *Reference Services in Academic Research Libraries.* (Chicago: American Library Association. Reference and Adult Services Division, 1986).

3. If a librarian works an eight-hour weekend shift on the reference desk every four weeks, her weekly average on the desk increases by two hours, or 5 percent assuming a 40-hour work week.

4. See Ferguson, "What Are You Doing?" p. 27; Emmerick, "A Survey," p. 94; Welch, "Are All Reference Jobs Created Equal?" p. 398.

5. Welch, p. 396; Charles Bunge, "Reference Desk Staffing Patterns: Report of a Survey," *RQ* 26 (Winter 1986): 175.

## Chapter 11

1. Mary Biggs and Victor Biggs, "Reference Collection Development in Academic Libraries: Report of a Survey," *RQ* 27 (Fall 1987): 69.

2. In making changes at UCSB, after the size of the collection was decided on, the number of stacks and best location were determined, and the collections in the area were weeded for deaccessioning or for putting into storage to provide the space.

3. Thomas Gwinup, "A Functional Arrangement of Indexes and Abstracts for the Humanities and the Social Sciences," *RQ* 13 (Winter 1973): 143–46.

4. Roger Horn, "Why They Don't Ask Questions," *RQ* 13 (Spring 1974): 225.

5. The standard article on reference collection policy is Kathleen Coleman and Pauline Dickinson, "Drafting a Reference Collection Policy," *College & Research Libraries* 38 (May 1977): 227–233. Development of reference collection policy statements is discussed and examples given in Bill Katz, *Reference and Online Services Handbook: Guidelines, Policies, and Procedures for Libraries*, vol. II (New York: Neal-Schuman, 1986).

6. The whole of issue no. 29 of *Reference Librarian* is devoted to "Weeding and Maintenance of Reference Collections," ed. by Sydney J. Pierce. *Reference Librarian* 29 (New York: Haworth Press, 1990).

7. Sometimes older reference works are useful for their historical value. For scholarship in the future, some older reference works should be kept somewhere. This may require the same kind of cooperation that the acquisition of rarely used materials requires.

8. Biggs and Biggs, p. 75.

9. Polly Frank, Lee-Allison Levene and Kathy Piehl, "Reference Collegiality: One Library's Experience," *Reference Librarian* 33 (1991): 41.

10. Different producers may issue the same database on CD-ROM. The user interface and search features will have to be considered in their selection.

11. Marie B. Waters, "Client-Driven Reference Collections for the 1990s," *Reference Librarian* 29 (1990): 93–102.

12. Fred W. Roper and Jo Anne Boorkman, *Introduction to Reference Sources in the Health Sciences* (Chicago: Medical Library Association, Inc., 1980), p. 4.

# *Chapter 12*

1. Recently the problem was discussed in Roma M. Harris, "Bibliographic Instruction: The Views of Academic, Special and Public Librarians," *College & Research Libraries* 53 (May 1992): 249. The most often cited article in support of answers rather than education has been Anita R. Schiller, "Reference Service: Instruction or Information," *Library Quarterly* 35 (Jan. 1965): 52–65. At that time she felt instruction was a secondary goal. In a later article (Anita R. Schiller, "Reference Instruction or Information," *Reference Librarian* 1/2 (Fall/Winter 1981): 3–11, she was much more in favor of instruction because of changes in demand for information and because instruction aims at making "libraries more usable, rather than less so"(p. 5). Joseph Rosenblum speaks out against instruction in his "Shifty Shoals of Bibliographic Instruction," *Journal of Academic Librarianship* 9 (Mar. 1983): 8–9. There are a number of pro-instruction papers in this same issue.

2. "The Future of Bibliographic Instruction: An Unresolved Issue" in

Anne Grodzins Lipow, ed., *Rethinking Reference in Academic Libraries* (Berkeley, Calif.: Library Solutions Press, 1993), pp. 124–51.

3. John C. Swan, "Librarians Are Still Teachers," *Library Journal* 108 (Sept. 1, 1983): 1624.

4. Rebecca R. Martin, "The Paradox of Public Service: Where Do We Draw the Line?," *College & Research Libraries* 51 (Jan. 1990): 25.

5. Samuel Rothstein, "Future Trends in the Development of Academic Reference Services," *Reference Librarian* 25/26 (1989): 401.

6. Joanne R. Euster, "'Full of Sound and Fury Signifying...' ... What?" *Journal of Academic Librarianship* 9 (March 1983): 14.

7. Carla Stoffle and Gabriella Bonn, "An Inventory of Library Orientation and Instruction Methods," *RQ* 13 (Winter 1973): 129–33.

8. Sonia Bodi, "Teaching Effectiveness and Bibliographic Instruction: The Relevance of Learning Styles," *College & Research Libraries* 51 (Mar. 1990): 113–19.

9. "A Commitment to Information Services: Developmental Guidelines," Section 1.5. *RQ* 18 (Spring 1979): 276.

10. Keith M. Cottam, "Avoiding Failure: Planning User Education," *RQ* 21 (Summer 1982): 331.

11. University of Texas at Austin, General Libraries, *A Comprehensive Program of User Education for the General Libraries, the University of Texas at Austin* (Austin, Texas, 1977).

12. "Guidelines for Bibliographic Instruction in Academic Libraries," as quoted by Patricia Breivik in *Planning the Library Instruction Program* (Chicago: American Library Association, 1982): 133–34 (Published originally in *College & Research Libraries News*, April 1977). There are also special guidelines for teaching online databases, including Dennis Hamilton, "Library Users and Online Systems: Suggested Objectives for Library Instruction," *RQ* 25 (Winter 1985): 195–97.

13. "Model Statement of Objectives for Academic Bibliographic Instruction: Draft Revision," *College & Research Libraries News* 48 (May 1987): 256–61.

14. Ron Blazek, "Effective Bibliographic Instruction Programs: A Comparison of Coordinators and Reference Heads in ARL Libraries," *RQ* (Summer 1985): 440–41.

15. Ellen Broidy, "Organizational Structure: Politics, Problems and Challenges," *RQ* 28 (Winter 1988): 162–68.

16. As examples, Breivik, *Planning*; John Lubans, *Educating the Library User* (New York: Bowker, 1974); Cerise Oberman and Katina Strauch, *Theories of Bibliographic Education: Designs for Teaching* (New York: R.R. Bowker, 1982); Anne K. Beaubien, Sharon A. Hogan and Mary W. George, *Learning the Library: Concepts and Methods for Effective Bibliographic Instruction* (New York: Bowker, 1982); the publications of the LOEX annual conference in the Library Orientation Series; Anne F. Roberts, *Organizing and Managing a Library Instruction Program* (Chicago: American Library Association, 1979); Marilla D. Svinicki and Barbara A. Schwartz, *Designing Instruction for Library Users: A Practical Guide* (New York: Marcel Dekker, Inc., 1988); and Constance A. Mellon, *Bibliographic Instruction: The Second Generation* (Littleton, Colo.:

Libraries Unlimited, 1987)—see notes on chapter one, pp. 17–23. There are also extensive bibliographies on library instruction updated yearly in *Reference Service Review*. Also, Deborah L. Lockwood, comp., *Library Instruction: A Bibliography* (Westport, Conn.: Greenwood Press, 1979).

17. *Library Instruction Clearing Houses, a Directory*. (Garden City, N.Y.: Adelphi University Swirbul Library, 1981-   ).

18. The Association of Research Libraries puts out SPEC kits for their members. Some of these will be on instructional topics. They will include examples from a number of different libraries.

19. The MELVYL system of the University of California has the ERIC index mounted on its catalog. The results of searches on ERIC can be printed or can be sent to a librarian's electronic mailbox.

20. BI-L is a computer conference dedicated to discussing ways of assisting library users effectively and efficiently. Contributors to the forum deal with the practical, theoretical and technical aspects of what has been called bibliographic instruction, library use instruction, library orientation and several other names. There is also LIBREF-L, a roundtable discussion among reference librarians. The latter is available on Internet as well as BITNET.

21. At UCSB, skills classes have been offered through the orientation program of the Educational Opportunity Program (primarily to minorities).

22. Candace R. Benefiel and Joe Jaros, "Planning and Testing a Self-Guided Taped Tour in an Academic Library," *RQ* 29 (Winter 1989): 199–208; Larry Hardesty, "Use of Slide-Tape Presentations in Academic Libraries: A State-of-the-Art-Survey," *Journal of Academic Librarianship* 3 (July 1977): 137–40.

23. For example, Ohio State University. Sandra Kerka, Deborah Murray and Arline Robbins, "LIP Service: The Undergraduate Library Instruction Program at the Ohio State University," *Journal of Academic Librarianship* 7 (November 1981): 279–82.

24. In the original program at UCLA.

25. In the original skills program at UCSB.

26. University of Minnesota.

27. For example, UCSB's *Library Skills* and *Library Research* textbooks as well as other textbooks have been published in ERIC.

28. Sonia Bodi, "Critical Thinking and Bibliographic Instruction: The Relationship," *Journal of Academic Librarianship* 14 (July 1988): 150–53. Linda Shirato, ed., *Judging the Validity of Information Sources: Teaching Critical Analysis in Bibliographic Instruction* (Ann Arbor, Mich.: Pierian Press, 1991).

29. Judy Johnson, "Applications of Learning Theory to Bibliographic Instruction: An Annotated Bibliography," *Research Strategies* 6 (Summer 1986): 138–41.

30. Pamela Kobelski and Mary Reichel, "Conceptual Frameworks for Bibliographic Instruction," *Journal of Academic Librarianship* 7 (May 1981): 73–77; Keith M. Cottam and Connie V. Dowell, "A Conceptual Planning Method for Developing Bibliographic Instruction Programs," *Journal of Academic Librarianship* 7 (Sept. 1981): 223–28; Betsy Baker, "A Conceptual Framework for Teaching Online Catalog Use," *Journal of Academic Librarianship* 12 (May 1986): 90–96.

31. Cerise Oberman and Rebecca A. Linton, "Guided Design: Teaching Library Research as Problem-Solving," in *Theories of Bibliographic Education: Designs for Teaching* (New York: Bowker, 1982): 111–34; Barbara Fister, "Teaching Research as a Social Act: Collaborative Learning and the Library," *RQ* 29 (Summer 1990): 505–09.

32. Carla J. Stoffle and Simon Karter, *Materials and Methods for History Research* (New York: Libraryworks, 1979); Carla J. Stoffle and others, *Materials and Methods for Political Science Research* (New York: Libraryworks, 1979).

33. William Kirk, "Problems in Library Instruction in Four-Year Colleges," in John Lubans, Jr., ed., *Educating the Library User*, (New York: Bowker, 1974): 83–103.

34. Instances might be tax materials, how a bill is enacted, or case law.

35. See Hardesty, "Use of Slide-Tape Presentations."

36. Two that come immediately to mind are on *Psychology Abstracts* and on citation indexes published by the Institute for Scientific Information.

37. In the future that may be less true, for faculty members will have acquired their Ph.D. making use of online systems.

38. Frederick Holler, "Towards a Reference Theory," *RQ* 14 (Summer 1975): 301–09.


# Chapter 13

1. At UCSB these two were the result of repeated assignments in classes in the history department.

2. Sally W. Kalin, "Support Services for Remote Users of Online Public Access Catalogs," *RQ* 31 (Winter 1991): 197–213.

3. Laurel G. Bowen and Peter J. Roberts, "Exhibits: Illegitimate Children of Academic Libraries?" *College & Research Libraries* 54 (September 1993): 407–15.


# Chapter 14

1. No. 11 of *Reference Librarian* (1984) was devoted to evaluation, and no. 38 of *Reference Librarian* (1992) was devoted to assessment and accountability in reference. A new edition of Lancaster's 1977 volume on reference was published in 1991: Sharon L. Baker and F. Wilfred Lancaster, *The Measurement and Evaluation of Library Services*, 2nd ed. (Arlington, Va.: Information Resources Press, 1991).

2. Samuel Rothstein, "The Measurement and Evaluation of Reference Services," *Library Trends* 12 (1964): 456–72; Terry L. Weech, "Evaluation of Adult Reference Services," *Library Trends* 22 (Jan. 1974): 316–35; Ronald R. Powell, "Reference Effectiveness: A Review of the Research," *Library and Information Science Research* 6 (Jan.–March 1984): 3–19; Marilyn Von Seggern, "Assessment of Reference Services," *RQ* 26 (Summer 1987): 487–96.

3. Von Seggern, "Assessment," p. 488.

4. Marjorie E. Murfin and Gary M. Gugelchuk, "Development of a Reference Transaction Assessment Instrument," *College and Research Libraries* 48 (July 1987): 315.

5. Baker, *Measurement and Evaluation*, p. 34.

6. Peter Hernon and Charles R. McClure, *Evaluation and Library Decision Making* (Norwood, N.J.: Ablex, 1990).

7. Robert S. Runyon, "The Library Administrator's Need for Measures of Reference," *RQ* 14 (Fall 1974): 10–11.

8. "Qualitative research methodology is designed to systematically and authoritatively examine effects rather than count items," writes Lynn Westbrook in *Qualitative Evaluation Methods for Reference Services: An Introductory Manual* (Washington D.C.: OMS, ARL, 1989), p. 1. Westbrook also discusses qualitative measurement methods in Lynn Westbrook, "Evaluating Reference: An Introductory Overview of Qualitative Methods," *Reference Service Review* 18 (Spring 1990): 73–78.

9. Powell itemizes both input and output measures in Ronald R. Powell, "Reference Effectiveness: A Review of Research," *Library and Information Science Research* 8 (Jan.–March 1984): 3–19. Hernon and McClure itemize input and output measures in areas amenable to evaluation in Peter Hernon and Charles R. McClure, *Unobtrusive Testing and Library Reference Services* (Norwood, N. J.: Ablex, 1987), pp. 8–10.

10. Ronald R. Powell, "An Investigation of the Relationships Between Quantifiable Reference Service Variables and Reference Performance in Public Libraries," *Library Quarterly* 48 (January 1978): 1–19.

11. Marjorie E. Murfin, "National Reference Measurement: What Can It Tell Us about Staffing?" *College & Research Libraries* 44 (Sept. 1983): 331.

12. Increasing a 250-volume collection by 250 would make a greater difference than increasing a 5,000-volume collection by 250.

13. Katz discusses ways of evaluating reference collections, William A. Katz, *Introduction to Reference Work*, Vol. II, 6th ed. (New York: McGraw-Hill, 1992).

14. Ellsworth Mason and Joan Mason, "The Whole Shebang—Comprehensive Evaluation of Reference Operations," *Reference Librarian* 11 (Fall/Winter 1984): 25–44.

15. Murfin, "National Reference Measurement," p. 326.

16. Ernest deProspo, Ellen Altman and Kenneth Beasley, *Performance Measures for Public Libraries* (Chicago: American Library Association, 1973); Paul B. Kantor, *Objective Performance Measures for Academic and Research Libraries* (Washington, D.C.: Association of Research Libraries, 1984).

17. Definitions can be found in *Library Information Handbook: A Handbook of Standard Terminology for Reporting and Recording Information About Libraries* (Boulder, Colo.: National Center for Higher Education Management Systems, 1979); Mary Jo Lynch, ed. *Library Data Collection Handbook* (Washington, D.C.: National Center for Educational Statistics, 1981).

18. For a long time the author felt inadequate when one of her colleagues always had hatch marks that indicated he helped twice as many patrons as she

did until she realized the statistics actually reflected how busy he thought he was. In similar circumstances, librarians who rarely accompany patrons to reference tools tend to have higher statistics because they are handling the quickie questions or providing superficial information.

19. Marjorie E. Murfin, "National Reference Measurement: What Can It Tell Us About Staffing?" *College & Research Libraries* 44 (Sept. 1983): 321–33.

20. Martin Kesselman and Sarah Barbara Watstein, "The Measurement of Reference and Information Services," *Journal of Academic Librarianship* 13 (March 1987): 24–30.

21. Marcella Ciucki, "Recording of Reference/Information Services Activities: A Study of Forms Currently Used," *RQ* 16 (Summer 1977): 273–283.

22. John P. Wilkinson and William Miller, "The Step Approach to Reference Services," *RQ* 17 (Summer 1978): 293–300.

23. Paul B. Kantor, "Quantitative Evaluation of the Reference Process," *RQ* 21 (Fall 1981): 43–52.

24. Peter Hernon and Charles R. McClure, "Library Reference Service: An Unrecognized Crisis," *Journal of Academic Librarianship* 13 (May 1987): 69–80; "The Continuing Debate on Reference Service: A Mini-Symposium," *Journal of Academic Librarianship* 13 (Nov. 1987): 278–284.

25. William Miller, "What's Wrong with Reference: Coping with Success and Failure at the Reference Desk," *American Libraries* 15 (May 1984): 303–306, 321–22.

26. Childers claims one-eighth in Thomas Childers, "The Quality of Reference: Still Moot After 20 Years," *Journal of Academic Librarianship* 13 (May 1987): 74; Whitlatch puts the number at 11.3 percent in Jo Beth Whitlatch, "Unobtrusive Studies and the Quality of Academic Library Service," *College & Research Libraries* 50 (May 1989): 182.

27. Childers, "The Quality of Reference," p. 73.

28. David Shavit, "Qualitative Evaluation of Reference Service," *Reference Librarian* 11 (Fall/Winter 1984): 235–44; Elizabeth Frick, "Qualitative Evaluation of User Education Programs: The Best Choice?" *Research Strategies* 8 (Winter 1990): 4–13.

29. Sydney Pierce, "In Pursuit of the Possible: Evaluating Reference Services," *Reference Librarian* 11 (Fall/Winter 1984): 9–21.

30. Hernon mentions areas to be studied in his *Evaluation and Library Decision Making*, p. 6.

31. Peter Hernon, "Utility Measures, Not Performance Measures for Library Reference Service?" *RQ* 26 (Summer 1987): 453.

32. Mignon S. Adams and Blanche Judd, "Evaluating Reference Librarians: Using Goal Analysis as a First Step," *Reference Librarian* 11 (Fall/Winter 1984): 131–145.

33. Jane P. Kleiner, "Ensuring Quality Reference Desk Service: The Introduction of a Peer Process," *RQ* 30 (Spring 1991): 349–361; Diane G. Schwartz and Dottie Eakin, "Reference Service Standards, Performance Criteria and Evaluation," *Journal of Academic Librarianship* 12 (Mar. 1986): 4–8.

34. Mary Jo Lynch, "Reference Interviews in Public Libraries," *Library Quarterly* 48 (Apr. 1978): 119–142.

35. Judith Mucci, "Videotape Self-Evaluation in Public Libraries: Experiments in Evaluating Public Service," *RQ* 16 (Fall 1976): 33–37; Marilyn Domas White, "Evaluation of the Reference Interview," *RQ* 25 (Fall 1985): 76–84.

36. White, "Evaluation of the Reference Interview," p. 77.

37. Elaine Z. Jennerich, "Before the Answer: Evaluating the Reference Process," *RQ* 19 (Summer 1980): 363.

38. Cheryl Elzy, Alan Nourie, E.W. Lancaster, and Kurt M. Joseph, "Evaluating Reference Service in a Large Academic Library," *College & Research Libraries* 52 (Sept. 1991): 454–65.

39. For a list of unobtrusive studies see F.W. Lancaster, *If You Want to Evaluate Your Library* (Champaign, Ill.: Graduate School of Library and Information Science, University of Illinois, 1988), pp. 112–113. Unobtrusive testing is also examined extensively in Peter Hernon and Charles R. McClure, *Unobtrusive Testing and Library Reference Services* (Norwood, N.J.: Ablex, 1987).

40. Richard Widdows, Tia A. Hensler, and Marlaya H. Wyncott, "The Focus Group Interview: A Method for Assessing Users' Evaluation of Library Service," *College & Research Libraries* 52 (July 1991): 352–359.

41. Benita J. Howell, Edward B. Reeves, and John Van Willigen, "Fleeting Encounters—A Role Analysis of Reference Librarian–Patron Interaction," *RQ* 16 (Winter 1976): 124–129; Murfin, "National Reference Measurement," pp. 321–333.

42. Murfin, "National Reference Measurement," pp. 321–333.

43. Lisa L. Smith, "Evaluating the Reference Interview: A Theoretical Discussion of the Desirability and Achievability of Evaluation," *RQ* 31 (Fall 1991): 78.

44. *Evaluating Bibliographic Instruction: A Handbook* (Chicago: American Library Association, College and Research Libraries, Bibliographic Instruction Section, 1983); Richard J. Beeler, Ed. *Evaluating Library Use Instruction*, Library Orientation Series, no. 4. (Ann Arbor, Mich.: Pierian Press, 1975).

45. Donald Barclay, "Evaluating Library Instruction: Doing the Best You Can with What You Have?" *RQ* 33 (Winter 1993): 195–202.

46. Roland Person, "Library Faculty Evaluation: An Idea Whose Time Continues to Come," *Journal of Academic Librarianship* 5 (July 1979): 143. McClure concurs with Person in claiming the primary reason for evaluation is the development of training programs and self improvement; see Charles R. McClure, "Output Measures, Unobtrusive Testing, and Assessing the Quality of Reference Services," *Reference Librarian* 11 (Fall/Winter 1984): 224.

47. William F. Young, "Evaluating the Reference Librarian," *Reference Librarian* 11 (Fall/Winter 1984): 123–129.

48. Mignon S. Adams and Blanche Judd, "Evaluating Reference Librarians: Using Goal Analysis as a First Step," *Reference Librarian* 11 (Fall/Winter 1984): 144.

49. Young states, "Part of the prescription [for improvement] may rest in improving the supervisory skills of reference managers." William F. Young, "Methods of Evaluating Reference Desk Performance," *RQ* 25 (Fall 1985): 74.

50. Pat Weaver-Meyers, "ARL Libraries and Staff Development: A Sug-

gested Model for Success," *College & Research Libraries* 51 (May 1990): 251–52.

51. For example, language training may result in collection development, cataloging and service in that language, and online searching skills contribute directly to the provision of this service. Advanced degrees in a subject field may create a better understanding of the research process and make it possible for the individual to give better service in that subject. In her experience with bibliographic instruction workshops, the author learned a great deal about how to present individual lessons which she later put into practice.

## Chapter 15

1. Charles Martell and Joan D. Kunselman, "QWL Strategies: Involvement-Commitment," *Journal of Academic Librarianship* 10 (July 1984): 158–60; Bob Perdue and Chris Piotrowski, "Supervisory Rotation: Impact on an Academic Library Staff," *RQ* 25 (Spring 1986): 361–65.

2. Steven E. Smith, "The Scheme," *American Libraries* 25 (October 1994): 865–66.

3. Anne Grodzins Lipow, *Rethinking Reference in Academic Libraries*, Proceedings and Process of Library Solutions Institute No. 2. (Berkeley, Calif.: Library Solutions Press, 1993), pp. 86–87.

4. These styles are discussed by Terry Mazany in Lipow, p. 25.

5. The principle is to run with the ball until you're tackled.

6. William Miller, "Logic and Passion at the Reference Desk," *Journal of Academic Librarianship* 11 (May 1985): 74.

7. Ron Blazek and Darlene Ann Parrish, "Burnout and Public Services: The Periodical Literature of Librarianship in the Eighties," *RQ* 31 (Fall 1992): 48–59; Nathan M. Smith, "Burnout: Fuel for the Fire. A Response to Bunge," *Journal of Academic Librarianship* 10 (July 1984): 133; Nathan M. Smith and Veneese C. Nelson, "Burnout: A Survey of Academic Reference Librarians," *College & Research Libraries* 44 (May 1983): 245–50.

8. Michael Argyle, *The Social Psychology of Work* (New York, Taplinger Publications, 1972), p. 20.

## Chapter 16

1. Diana M. Thomas, Ann T. Hinckley and Elizabeth R. Eisenback, *The Effective Reference Librarian* (New York: Academic Press, 1981), p. 1.

2. Ron Blazek and Darlene Ann Parrish, "Burnout and Public Services: The Periodical Literature of Librarianship in the Eighties," *RQ* 31 (Fall 1992): 48–59; Nathan M. Smith, "Burnout: Fuel for the Fire. A Response to Bunge," *Journal of Academic Librarianship* 10 (July 1984): 133; Nathan M. Smith and Veneese C. Nelson, "Burnout: A Survey of Academic Reference Librarians," *College & Research Libraries* 44 (May 1983): 245–50.

3. As quoted by Keith Cottam, "Professional Attitudes, Productive Roles: Roads to Achievement," in Sul H. Lee, ed. *Reference Service: A Perspective* (Ann Arbor, Mich., The Pierian Press, 1983), p. 54.

4. S. D. Neill, "Problem Solving and the Reference Process," *RQ* 14 (Summer 1975): 310–15. "The Reference Process and Certain Types of Memory: Semantic, Episodic, and Schematic," *RQ* 23 (Summer 1984): 417–23.

5. *Webster's Collegiate Dictionary*, 5th ed. (Springfield, Mass.: G. & C. Merriam Co., 1948), p. 497.

6. Anne Grodzins Lipow, ed. *Rethinking Reference in Academic Libraries* (Berkeley, Calif.: Library Solutions Press, 1993), p. 55.

7. Cottam, "Professional Attitudes."

## Chapter 17

1. Charles A. D'Aniello, "Cultural Literacy and Reference Service," *RQ* 28 (Spring 1989): 370–80.

2. Jose-Marie Griffiths and Donald W. King, *New Directions in Library and Information Science Education* (White Plains, N.Y.: Knowledge Industry Publications, Inc., for the American Society for Information Science, 1986); Lawrence W. S. Auld, "The King Report: New Directions in Library and Information Science Education," *College & Research Library News* 48 (April 1987): 174–79.

3. Thomas, *The Effective Reference Librarian*, p. 2.

4. Herbert S. White, "Defining Basic Competencies," *American Libraries* 14 (Sept. 1983): 520.

5. John C. Larsen, "Information Sources Currently Studied in General Reference Courses," *RQ* 18 (Summer 1979): 341–48.

6. Zheng Fan with Nancy Slater, "Reference Queries, Experience, and Secondary Reference Books," *Reference Librarian* 22 (1988): 271–82.

7. James R. Parrott, "Simulation of the Reference Process, Part II: REF-SIM, an Implementation with Expert System and ICAI Model," *Reference Librarian* 23 (1989): 153–75.

8. "Californians Peg Entry Level Librarian I 'Tasks,'" *Library Journal* 102 (Nov. 15, 1977): 2298, 2300; Jose-Marie Griffiths, "Our Competencies Defined: A Progress Report and Sampling," *American Libraries* 15 (Jan. 1984): 43–45.

9. White discusses when certain things should be learned in his article "Defining Basic Competencies," *American Libraries* 14 (Sept. 1983): 519–25.

10. White, "Defining Basic Competencies," p. 525.

11. Compare Cottam, "Professional Attitudes," pp. 58–59.

## Chapter 19

1. "Californians Peg Entry Level Librarian I 'Tasks,'" *Library Journal* 102 (Nov. 15, 1977): 2298, 2300; Jose-Marie Griffiths, "Our Competencies

Defined: A Progress Report and Sampling," *American Libraries* 15 (Jan. 1984): 43–45.

2. Herbert S. White discusses when certain things should be learned in his article "Defining Basic Competencies," *American Libraries* 14 (Sept. 1983): 519–25.

3. Beth S. Woodward, "A Selective Guide to Training Literature for the Reference Librarian/Trainer," *RSR Reference Service Review* 17 (Summer 1989): 41–51.

4. Roberta J. Walters and Susan J. Barnes, "Goals, Objectives, and Competencies for Reference Service: A Training Program at the UCLA Biomedical Library," *Bull. Med. Libr. Assoc.* 73 (Apr. 1985): 160–67.

5. The appendix to the article identifies twelve objectives and lists competencies for each. Walters, "Goals," pp. 162–67.

6. Donnagene Britt, ed. *Painlessly Preparing Personalized Training Plans* (University of California at Berkeley, General Library, 1982).

7. These are spelled out in "Model Statement of Criteria and Procedures for Appointment, Promotion in Academic Rank, and Tenure for College and University Librarians," *College & Research Libraries News* 48 (May 1987): 247–54.

8. "Faculty Status: 2001," *College & Research Libraries News* 54 (June 1993): 338–40.

9. "Standards for Faculty Status for College and University Librarians," *College & Research Libraries News* 53 (May 1992): 317–18.

10. Charles B. Lowry, "The Status of Faculty Status for Academic Librarians: A Twenty-Year Perspective," *College & Research Libraries* 54 (March 1993): 170.

11. For example, at UCSB, a librarian was recently appointed to the Committee on Effective Teaching and Instructional Support.

12. For example, the American Library Association, College and Research Libraries, state library organizations, the Special Libraries Association, the Art Libraries Association, clearinghouses for library instruction such as LOEX or the California Clearinghouse, online searching organizations, and professional subject organizations, such as the American Psychological Association or the Modern Language Association.

13. For example, Cerise Oberman, having achieved success in her library research classes, has published articles and books and has given preconference continuing education classes for the Association of College and Research Libraries at the ALA conventions.

14. A list of workshops sponsored by the California Clearinghouse on Library Education or LOEX, preconferences sponsored by ACRL at ALA, or workshops of the California Academic and Research Libraries Group could indicate the variety of topics.

15. William K. Black and Joan M. Leysen, "Scholarship and the Academic Librarian," *College & Research Libraries* 55 (May 1994): 229–41.

16. Patricia Gebhard, "Continuing Education in the '80s: Thoughts of a Service Librarian," in Nancy Fjallbrant, ed., *Education for Work in Technological University Libraries, IATUL Proceedings* 13 (1981): 71–75.

17. Samuel Rothstein, "Future Trends in the Development of Academic Reference Service," *Reference Librarian* 25/26 (Sept. 1989): 396–409.

18. This author took her first library course on a staff scholarship from the University of Minnesota. At UCSB librarians have either had time off granted to pursue graduate studies or have taken them on their own time depending on circumstances.

19. "Think Tank Recommendations for Bibliographic Instruction," *College & Research Libraries News* 42 (Dec. 1981): 396.

20. Evan Farber, Sharon Hogan, and Carla Stoffle among others have presented memorable workshops.

21. John Lubans, ed., *Educating the Library User* (New York: Bowker, 1974); Cerise Oberman and Katina Strauch, eds., *Theories of Bibliographic Education: Designs for Teaching* (New York: Bowker, 1982); Constance A. Mellon, *Bibliographic Instruction: The Second Generation* (Littleton, Colo.: Libraries Unlimited, 1987); Deborah L. Lockwood, comp., *Librarian Instruction: A Bibliography* (Westport, Conn.: Greenwood Press, 1979).

22. Roy Tennant, *Crossing the Internet Threshold: An Instructional Handbook* (Berkeley, Calif.: Library Solutions Press, 1993); Brendan P. Kehoe, *Zen and the Art of the Internet: A Beginner's Guide*, 2nd ed. (Englewood Cliffs, N.Y. (PTR Prentice Hall, 1993); "A Hands-On Introduction to the Internet," Workshop, Fall 1993, California State University, Fullerton.

23. On Novell at UC Berkeley, the census CDs can be mounted and accessed from various localities. At UCSB, the campus has a file of experimental courses that have been offered on its network, and the library offers information and news on the local network.

24. Roberta J. Walters, "Goals, Objectives, and Competencies for Reference Service: A Training Program at the UCLA Biomedical Library," *Bull. Med. Libr. Assoc.* 73 (April 1985): 160-67.

25. Circulation of literature is a problem because of the time it takes and because while a given issue of a magazine is circulating, no one knows where to find it.

# Index

187